Grhaham James
Happy birthday :
back to the age

7.2.2013

THE
PILKINGTON
GENE

Joe McCall

Visit us online at www.authorsonline.co.uk

A Bright Pen Book

Copyright © Joseph McCall

All rights reserved. No part of this publication may be reproduced, stored in a retrieval system, or transmitted in any form or by any means, electronic, mechanical, photocopy, recording or otherwise, without prior written permission of the copyright owner. Nor can it be circulated in any form of binding or cover other than that in which it is published and without similar condition including this condition being imposed on a subsequent purchaser.

ISBN 978- 0-7552-1331-3

Authors OnLine Ltd
19 The Cinques
Gamlingay, Sandy
Bedfordshire SG19 3NU
England

This book is also available in e-book format
details of which are available at www.authorsonline.co.uk

Contents

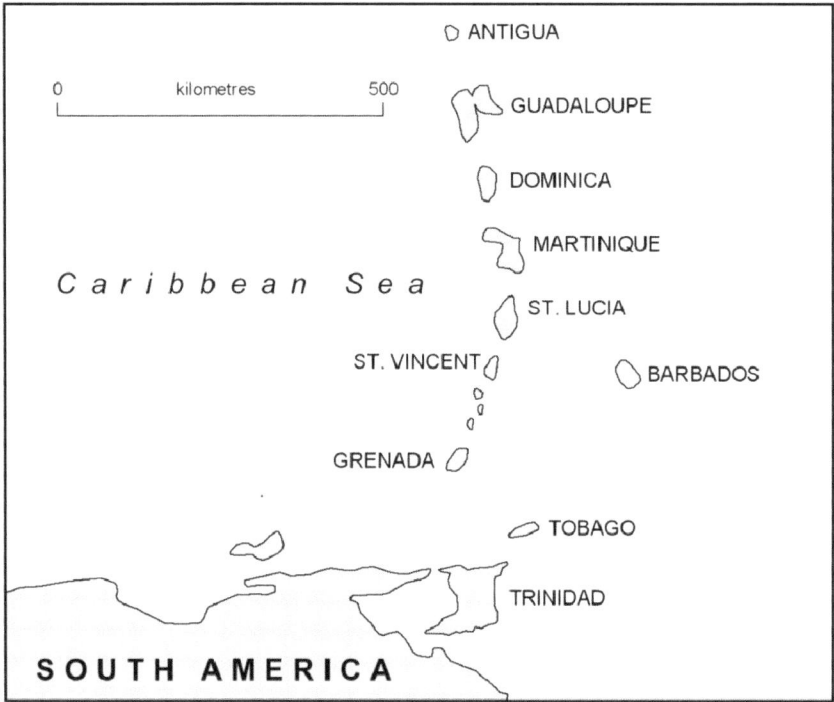

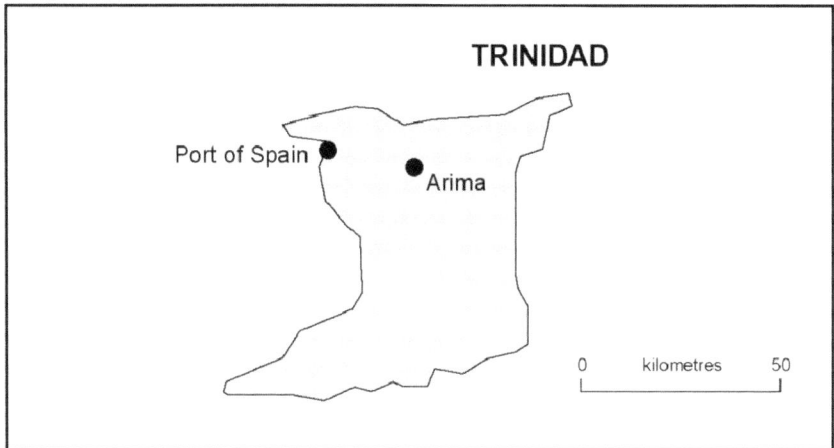

1. Sketch map of the West Indies showing where George Pilkington was active in the Napoleonic Wars and later from 1822-1830 in Trinidad.

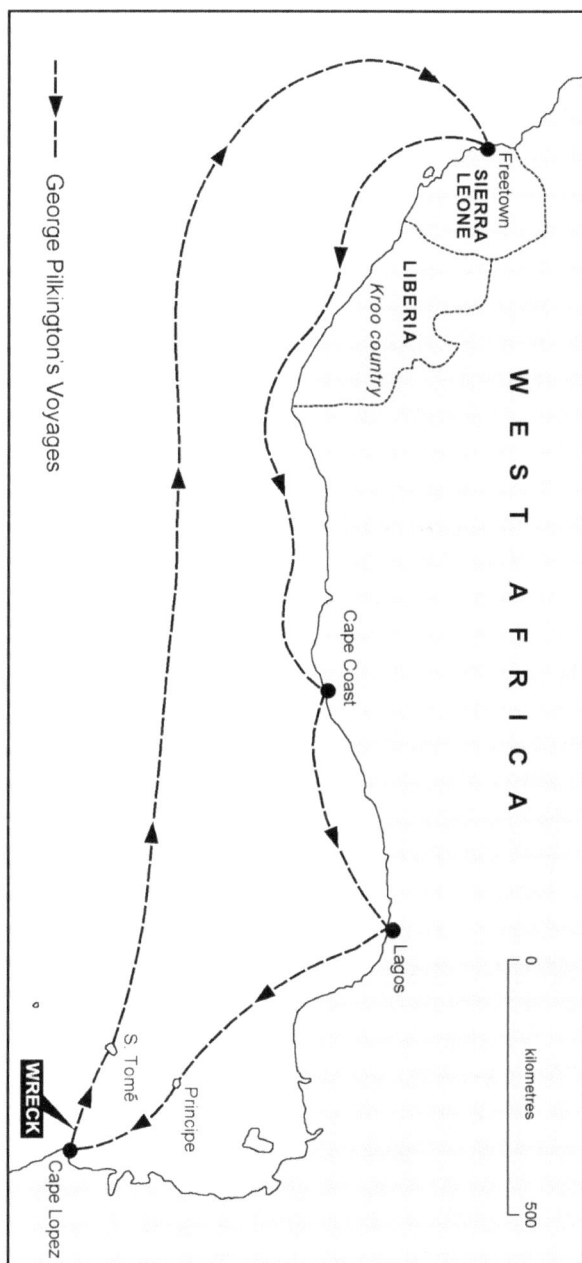

2. Sketch map of West Africa showing where George Pilkington served in Sierra Leone from 1816-1820 and the places visited in his ill-fated coastal trading venture.

3. Map of the area in the Shetlands on which George Pilkington travelled during his stay there.

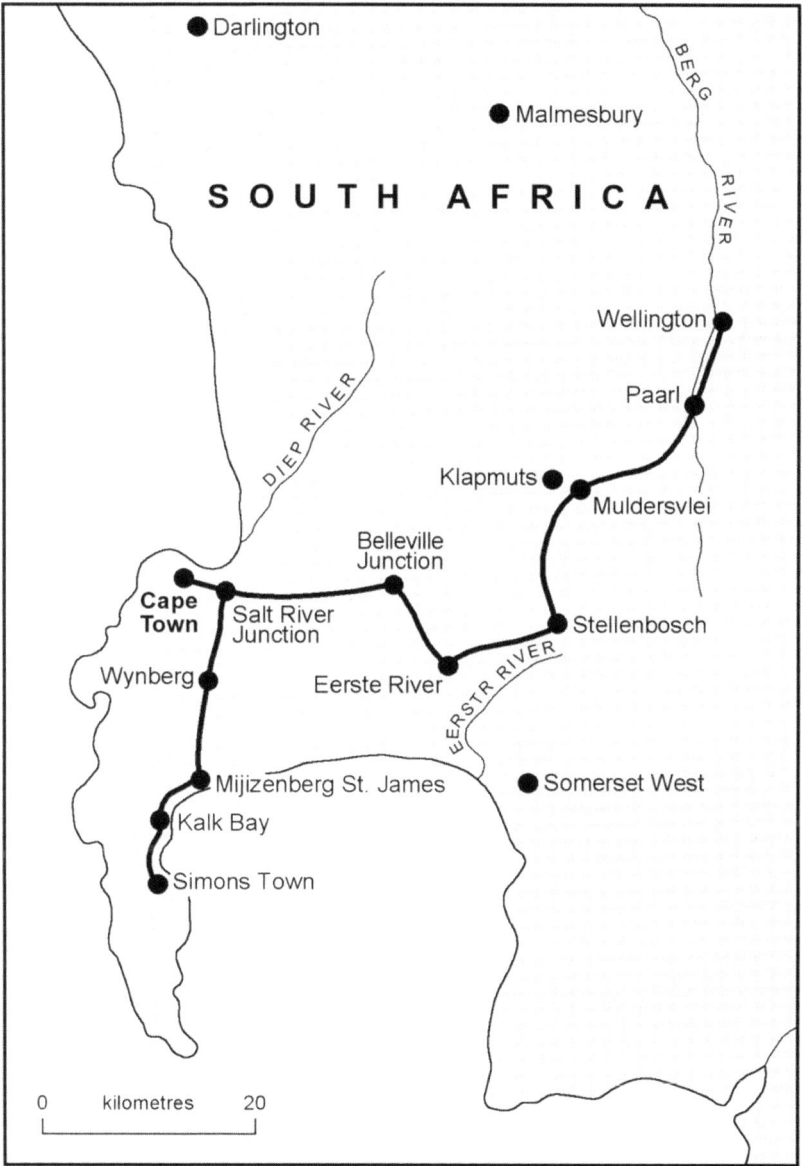

4. Sketch map of the route of the first railway in the Cape, surveyed by George Pilkington in 1857, completed by Woodford Pilkington, from Cape Town to Paarl and Wellington.

THE PILKINGTON 'GENE'

A memoir of George Pilkington, my great-great grandfather

Joe McCall

1. Preface

Though I have been involved as author or editor in the publication of nearly twenty books, they have all been related to my sixty years spent as a professional geologist on five continents, so this memoir is a new departure. My forebears have been a source of inspiration throughout a long life: my mother's side being a particularly rich source for her father, Joseph Kidd, born in Limerick in 1824 was the 17th of a family of 20. He himself had fifteen offspring; his second wife was one of a family of 15 and he had a most interesting life as a consultant physician. He tended medically the Irish Potato famine at Bantry and Skull for the Homoeopathic Society and later was Benjamin Disraeli's consultant physician.

My father was secretive about his ancestry though it has been worked out on his father's side back to one John MacCall or MacAla, a 'stockenmaker' born at Ayr in 1731. But the rich store in my father's case is the story of the Ballantyne Press and Vale Press (managed successively by his father, Charles, and himself, Charles Home), which around 1900 produced the entire works of Shakespeare among other fine works. This story is well covered in "The Vale Press" by Maureen Watry (2004). I have written about all these in an autobiography, entitled "Thank God for Life", the two volumes of which will probably end up in the archives of the Geological Society of which I am a Senior Fellow of 60 years membership.

In 2006-2007, I made contact with Peter Kidd, my eldest uncle, Percy Kidd's, great grandson. Peter has produced an excellent family tree of the Kidd's and surprisingly, the Rouse's, the family of my maternal grandmother, to whom he himself is not related because Joseph Kidd married twice; his first wife Sophia Mackern died and leaving him with eight children; he then married Fanny Octavia Rouse when he was 51 and she 18, and there were seven more children of this second marriage, of whom my mother was the fourth, and twelfth in Joseph's family. Joseph Kidd died at the age of 95 in 1918, two years before I was born in 1920, as my mother's seventh and last child: hence my name, Joseph.

When given an award (the 'Coke medal') by the Geological Society in 1994, I mentioned the fact that I have been blessed by serendipity in my Geological career. Serendipity appeared once again in my life when Peter Kidd opened up a quite unexpected seam of richness in my ancestry. My mother often talked about George Pilkington; I knew there were Pilkington cousins, for one, 'Catalina' (Kathleen) Pilkington, a middle-aged lady used to come to Hastings where we lived in the 1930's and take out my sister Janey, my brother Terence and me on delightful excursions: she was unmarried, but had a wonderful way with children. I never connected her to my great grandmother, Fanny's mother, who was Clara Pilkington according to Peter Kidd's researches. Clara was the daughter of George Pilkington, born 1785 in Dublin but related distantly to the well-known Lancashire family from Bolton. They apparently were a Protestant family in Westmeath and indeed still are reported to operate a tile business in Mullingar.

For some years I had carried in my study a book by him, published in 1839: this had been put in a collection of unwanted family bibles and other oddments passed down to me, mainly derived from thrown-away objects at family homes after family deaths. I also once met George Pilkington Mills, the legendary cyclist associated with the Liverpool Cycling Club and Raleigh, who is still the subject of 'Google' entries; I met him at Hastings during the 1930's: like 'Catalina' he was a grandchild of George Pilkington. In hospital nurses always remark that I have in my eighties the heart of a young man, so perhaps this physical inheritance came down in the Pilkington genes, like the case of George Mills who performed incredible physical endurance feats on an early 'ordinary' ('penny-farthing') bicycle! George Pilkington himself, as the reader will discover, must have been endowed with an equally immense stamina.

I opened George Pilkington's 1839 book with new interest and it led me to purchase at a great price his earlier 1836 book from a bookseller in Reading. Here was the story of a quite remarkable man – eccentric to the n'th degree and clearly a frequent problem with his very definite opinions to his employers as an engineer in the Military and Civil spheres. My mother always said the Rouse's had no common sense and this is vindicated by the fact that Great Uncle Martin Luther Rouse (a strong protestant and liberal streak in his mother had led her to opt for this naming, in preference to Oliver Cromwell Rouse!) reportedly committed bigamy (this may be untrue, but he was as she wrote 'always out of step with ordinary men and devoted his life to a series of crusades of a useless and negligible type, his final unfulfilled ambition being to lead an expedition to discover the remains of Noah's Ark on Mount Ararat!') His sister, Great Aunt Edith Rouse, besides collecting two husbands legally, was so bird-witted that she once went out and bought forty hats at one shopping spree!

A strong strain of originality, verging on eccentricity, can be detected in my generation and those that come afterwards, and I attribute it to George Pilkington's genes, which some of my foolish Rouse great-uncles and great-aunts possessed. My grandmother, née Frances Octavia Rouse, was also prone to foolish fancies

3

including the idea that the bronze statue of Queen Victoria at St Leonards-on Sea should be equipped with an umbrella to keep off the damage by sea-gulls' droppings! She wrote to the local paper suggesting this! She also, after Joseph Kidd died, erected a remarkable dwelling in the style of Hampton Court at Hastings called 'John's Place'. All her legacy went on this and she had to sell it and live in a smaller Victorian residence, No 1 Havenside, De Cham Rd, which was ever threatening to collapse down a steep hillside like Mrs Clennam's in Little Dorritt. John's Place became the Municipal Museum and housed the Indian Darbar collections of Brassey, the Indian railway magnate, who resided in retirement near Hastings. It also housed some of the fake birds and fossils of Charles Dawson, the Piltdown perpetrator.

Beyond his eccentricity there was a nobleness in George, especially in his concern for the coloured people in the West Indies and West Africa and his self-imposed Wesley-type religious lecturing all over Britain, a nobleness that shines through his improbable life story. He was also undoubtedly a talented engineer. His books are tortuous to present day readers with interpolated religious texts and digressions: so I have tried here to extract the best from accounts of his extraordinary life.

....

2. Beginnings

George Pilkington was born at Camden Street, Dublin, in 1785 (some records have his birthday as March 1784 or 1786, but it is reasonable to suppose that he would have his birth year correct in his writings). He descended from the well-known Lancashire family – there are records of Pilkington merchants at Bury in 1462 and at Salford in 1498 – some of them emigrated to Ireland, where the surname is very common. His mother was Irish and had the surname Dickson. His father is listed as George William Pilkington of Urney, Westmeath. As the family lived in Camden Street, Dublin, it is reasonable to assume that they were small gentry with a country and town property, but it is possible that his father, whom he refers to as 'having many afflictions', lost his property in the insurrection in Westmeath in 1798. His father's occupation is unknown, but he was buried at the age of 47 about 1814 in St Peter's Churchyard, Dublin: George visited the site in 1837 when he referred to his 'honoured father' and his 'many afflictions'. His brothers and a sister were already buried there also by this time. He had not seen his father since parting 'at the Quay' 33 years before.

The family must have been reasonably well-off for George went to Trinity College, Dublin, after spending nine years at a large grammar school in the city. However, he quitted university in 1804, at the age of 19, for the purpose of accepting a commission in the Royal Engineers which was tendered to him through a relative then in that department of the military service (his uncle, General Cunningham). He was surely not qualified as an Engineer by then but there was at that time a greater demand for scientific men than the Military College could supply. He must have picked up his engineering skills in the service; we know that he went to Woolwich Military Academy.

The profession 'seemed congenial to my youthful disposition, having been brought up in that mistaken mode where boys are encouraged to seek for such amusements amongst their fellows to stimulate the mind to a love of fighting and a passion for bold and daring enterprises. These tendencies, under the misguided influence of a law of honour, were in Ireland so generally deemed desirable, that parents were accustomed to laud praise on their children [who were] conspicuous for a high spirited conduct'. He also says in his second book that, 'in consequence of seeing that Christians engage in wars, and contend against each other, while on both sides claiming Christ's assistance, I became an infidel, and

5

entered His Majesty's military service in 1804'. He adds that it is not to be wondered that, at that time 'to the peaceful arts, he greatly preferred and gladly embraced the profession of arms'.

The Pilkington family of Lancashire may, I believe, have had Quaker connections, like my grandfather Joseph Kidd's mother and father, but it appears that George Pilkington's family were Protestants by 1785, when he was christened.

He had witnessed with disgust the conduct of professing Christians around him during the rebellion of 1798 - men who were 'mutually engaged in the revolting work of slaughtering each other, as they affirmed in Christian principles and for Christian objects.' He witnessed bitter animosity, dreadful carnage and hideous cruelty on both sides - this echoes the much later activities of the Black and Tans and opposing nationalists, the civil war in Ireland, and both sides in the 'Troubles ' recently ended in Northern Ireland: will Ireland ever be free from this mindless violence?

5. Trinity College , Dublin, where George Pilkington spent a short time, before joining the Royal Engineers: Photographed by Joe McCall, 1998, at a meeting of the Meteoritical Society.

3. Service in the West Indies

George Pilkington joined the Royal Engineers and left in 1814 with the rank of Captain., his services 'being dispensed with by the Duke of York' (he who marched them up the hill and down again). He reported a Major General for peculation. The circumstances are a bit obscure, but, reading between the lines, George must have been involved in construction of quarters in Antigua, officially for the general's ADC, but which the General took for himself. It is an extraordinary story, for, as George wrote, the disgrace attached to the general (he is named as W.P. C---y), who was subject to a court martial in Barbados, 350 sea miles away, but held his position, having only to refund the money, whereas George was dismissed from the service. The Army List wrongly stated that he was 'cashiered', and George 'never bothered to correct this'. In fact he was not subjected to any court martial himself, a requirement for cashiering, and was subsequently appointed by the Master-general, Lord Mulgrave, as Chief Civil Engineer, Sierra Leone. A person cashiered cannot serve the Crown in any capacity again. He was allowed passage money from Antigua to Dominica via Barbados (£30), expenses of evidence (£300) and the cost of his passage home from the West Indies.

The court's verdict on the General clearly found him guilty of one charge. Extract of the opinion and sentence of the court:

> *As to the 5th charge, the court is the opinion that the Commander of the Forces was induced to order a house to be built at the expense of the public, for Major-General C-'s servants, by the Major-General reporting that he had not sufficient accommodation for them and that he appropriated the said building for his Aid-de-Camp, Lieutenant Forbes; and the court is of the opinion that the Major-General did sanction the use of lodging money in the name, and to the receipt of his Aid-de Camp, in the*

usual manner that it is obtained for the hire of lodging, when a King's quarter cannot be furnished, in order to obtain that allowance for himself; and that he did actually obtain it, instead of the Aid-de-Camp, and appropriate it to his own use; and therefore, the court finds this part of the charge proved,

The court also finds that a return was made for lodging money for Lieutenant Forbes, the Major-General's Aid-de-Camp , during his absence in Antigua, and that the Major-General did receive the amount of such lodging money; but at the same time, it appears to the court that such return was not made by the Major-General as a false muster; and therefore the court does not conceive that it comes under the head of, or can be considered as, a false muster within any of the Articles of War, and doth therefore acquit Major-General C- of this part of the charge.

The court having thus given its opinion on these several charges, doth sentence and adjudge, that Major-General C- do refund to the Government all the money received for his Aid-de-Camp, Lieutenant Forbes, whilst he was stationed in Antigua. The court cannot but conceive that the Major-General as extremely reprehensible for not having informed himself of his right to receive such lodging money, when he might, had he thought proper, to have so easily procured necessary information on the subject; and the court do further sentence and adjudge, for such his neglect, he be reprimanded in such a manner as His Excellency, the Commander of the Forces , shall see meet.

George wrote that not a single officer, with the exception of those close to the Commander-in-Chief, was not shocked by this decision. However, the establishment will always rally around the establishment in such cases. George was aged 29 at the time of this crisis in his life, and was, perhaps, impetuous. If George Pilkington had remained in the Royal Engineers in the West Indies, he would not have gone on to his extraordinary adventures in West Africa where he gained his insight into the evils of slavery, nor served his term as a Civil Engineer in Trinidad where his religious ideas developed and he was active against slavery, and followed his next occupation as a preacher/lecturer against slavery, the evils of war, drink and other topics throughout the British Isles.

He admits in a footnote, written in his second book after he took up religious evangelism, that he could have done nothing, and remained in his position in the Army, for he now perceived that 'the true policy of Christian principle directs us to resist not evil, but to overcome evil with good'. However, this would have meant to 'patiently endure injury and insult'

The final word on this matter must rest with Major General, William Johnstone, and Colonel of the Royal Engineers, which testifies both to George Pilkington's excellent qualities as an engineer, and strongly deprecates the outcome of the Court Martial of the General, leading to his dismissal. It also notes that he had a quick temper, something that must surely have been controlled as he became older and wiser, and took up evangelism. This letter unquestionably ensured his subsequent civil appointment as Chief Engineer in Sierra Leone.

William Johnstone's letter:

> *Barbadoes, March 1, 1814*
>
> *To Lieut-General Mann,*
> *Inspector-General &c., &c., &c.*
>
> *Having, on the 11th of February, the day after I received your communication, put into the hands of Captain Pilkington, the letter containing the command of the Prince*

Regent, and Master-General of Ordnance;   I feel powerfully impelled to lend the aid of my testimony to the merits and unfortunate situation in which that gentleman now finds himself placed, who, most unexpectedly now stands far from his native country, and without fortune or friends, except such as the character of the gentleman and an officer unimpeachd may have attached to him.. I, Sir, have known Mr. Pilkington intimately since his arrival in this country some years ago, in all the situations of duty in which he had been placed; and it is not too much for me to say, that in all and every one, whether on service, or in the more retired situation of a stationary officer of the corps, he has evinced zeal and abilities of the very first promise.

That Mr. Pilkington has an impetuosity of temper, which sometimes places a young man, whose sense of honour and injury is above control in critical situations, I have not even inclination to controvert; most dearly, in the present instance, has he suffered by it.
My having been a member of the court-martial, on which Captain Pilkington was the prosecutor, prevents me from saying much, which I should be prompted to urge under any other circumstances; yet I cannot but deeply lament his untimely fate, and the real loss the service sustains in a young man, than I know none that has promised in ability, zeal, and intelligence more to uphold the honour and credit of the corps.

I have the honour to be, Sir,
Your very obedient servant,
William Johnstone
Major-General and Colonel of the Royal Engineers

Following this event George returned to England in 1814. We do not know with what he occupied himself during the next two years, but he did get married at St. Brides, Fleet Street, to Charlotte Jollie, daughter of Thomas William Jollie, an expert in privateers and turkey dealer. She was born in Blackheath in 1800, so she was only 16 years old when she married George.

He had actually served with some distinction, attached to the 8th West Indian Regiment, being present at the capture of Martinique and Guadeloupe in 1809 and 1810, later commander of the engineers on St Kitts, where a French attack was repulsed: he received the thanks of George III for this. He was a prisoner of war of the French from September 1807 to April 1808. In 1811 he prepared the general plan for the military position in Antigua, and it must have been this task which brought him into trouble, recognising the General's misuse of funds.

6. Antigua: Officers quarters from old colonial days. This was the main English naval base in the Napoleonic wars and Nelson spent several years there: it was very unhealthy, yellow fever being endemic. He described it as 'a vile place', and 'a dreadful hole' George Pilkington was presumably improving such buildings there when he discovered the misuse of funds by a general, in the construction of his quarters there. William IV, when Duke of Clarence was also there at the time, but in more comfortable quarters, 'Clarence House'.

7. Vanbrugh Castle, a folly in Greenwich Park. Charlotte Pilkington's father (surname Jollie) resided there and as he is described as a turkey-breeder, maybe kept the turkeys there? In one of the Sherlock Holmes stories it is clear that Turkeys were bred for Christmas in the 19th Century in suburban backyards.

4. To Sierra Leone

George Pilkington, now aged 32, sailed with his wife to Sierra Leone in 1817. As Chief Civil Engineer, West Coast of Africa, he supervised the erection of many buildings in various towns, and had many opportunities to observe the 'Free Blacks', whom he found intelligent and docile. He witnessed their deportment on the bench as magistrates – as pleaders at the bar and grand and petty jurors. He had reason to admire the upright, faithful and conscientious mode in which they discharged the duties of these offices. Neither of the two individuals practising as solicitors or attorneys had been professionally trained, one was a European who acted as Kings Advocate to the Vice-Admiralty Court and the other a 'person of colour', born and educated in England, and engaged in mercantile pursuits. 'Nothing can more indisputably prove the tranquillity of this settlement containing 22,000 inhabitants, than the fact that there were only two lawyers there and even these could not gain their subsistence from their professional employment alone'.

The 'Sierra Leone' was named by a Portuguese explorer, Pedro de Sintra in 1462, because he heard thunder in the mountains which resembled a lion's roar. The settlement was made by those removed from Nova Scotia, 'Maroons' from Jamaica; those liberated from slave ships, and a few from adjacent tribes: all these 'people of colour'. There were about fifty English people there, civil and military officers, religious teachers, merchants and mechanics. The settlers were chiefly involved in trading speculations. The colony had been attacked by the French in 1794, but not at any other time.

I myself visited Freetown in early 1942, when our convoy, heading to occupy Madagascar, refuelled in the bay for three days. We were not allowed ashore; on one side were the hills of great beauty, swathed in green vegetation, on the other flat mangrove swamps. It was extremely oppressive with heat by day, and the only sign of life was the daily train which passed our mooring (the famous train to Bo, which according to the rhyme, 'does not go').

This coast was subject to malaria, bilharzia and sleeping sickness, and it was a saying among seamen that 'in the Bay of Benin, one came out when forty went in'. The unhealthy climate was what caused George Pilkington to move on. The climate seriously and 'injuriously' afflicted George Pilkington's wife, Charlotte, and himself, and after two and a half years, he relinquished his civil employment. Two of his wife's brothers had died there, and one of his deceased relatives had bequeathed him a small amount of merchandise from his mercantile pursuits, so George purchased a prize vessel that was in the harbour, and decided to undertake a trading voyage along the coast, leaving his wife in Freetown.

His first voyage was up the Rio Pongas visiting the 'Timini and Sussro Nations', and he sailed up the Kissi River as far as it was navigable for the vessel, and then reached its source by the boat. He visited the Mandingo natives, who require by custom that the visitor states his purpose, and then he is safe from 'penal enactment' of their laws. This custom he found prevalent throughout the West African coast. These people are Mahommedans, and have a law that no 'bookman' (one carrying the Koran) shall be sold as a slave. They constantly read the Koran and carry it with them as a token of their privileges.

His next voyage took him southward, touching on the Kroo country (present day Liberia) where he found a hardy, active, intelligent race of men devoted to labour and agricultural pursuits. They cultivated white rice when in season. It was difficult there to obtain access to the interior, and this cut them off from the odious slave trade (the easiest and most infamous means of obtaining a livelihood). These people single-handedly navigated small canoes to Sierra Leone (a distance of 120 leagues), to obtain employment. The canoes were fashioned out of a single piece of soft wood, and were so light that they could be stored in the roofs of the houses. They were propelled with a 2 ft long paddle, held with both hands. They sold large quantities of rice, transported in small amounts in these canoes to visiting vessels. They were familiar with several local dialects, also the English, French and Dutch languages. Pilkington notes that no Krooman shall be sold as a slave, and in his 18 years in the West Indies he never saw a single Kroo slave.

He next visited Cape Coast Castle (in present day Ghana), where the Ashantee were threatening an incursion. The civil governor had heard that he was coming and his secretary came on board and asked him to dine at the castle. All his officers, including civil appointees wore military uniform. The settlement was the property of a commercial company, but even the officers of this company held military rank. He lodged at the fort and breakfasted with the Governor at his country house, being transported there in a splendid carriage with small wheels and a hand pole; this was drawn by four young men dressed in loose trousers, drawn at the knee, and glazed hats. Belts passed over their shoulders; the two at the rear operated a drag-pole, like a tiller on a ship. Horses were not used, reportedly because the herbage disagreed with them, but George Pilkington suspected that 'the free blacks did not greatly desire the rivalship of quadrupeds to disturb their monopoly of labour', employment being scarce.

He surveyed the neighbouring country in order to site a Martello Tower, having been invited to plan this. This task occupied him for 3 weeks. It was called Phipps' Tower, according to his account (though Phipps' Tower appears to have been an 18th C erection, gone into dereliction by the time George visited the castle). His fortification has later been attributed to the successful resistance of a ferocious Ashantee descent. There are two towers near Cape Coast

15

Castle, Fort William and Fort Victoria. The former was built in 1820 which fits in with George's account, but Fort Victoria also appears to have the form of a Martello tower, and George may have planned either. They were used as look-outs for the main castle, and Fort William was later used as a lighthouse.

He notes in his first book, written years later, that with his present Christian outlook he believed that Christians should not have provoked the Ashantee by taking unlawful advantage of them.

He then sailed to Lagos and hired a canoe with 6 paddle men and a pilot to take him across the bar to the river. This was expensive, but was compensated by advantageous purchase of 'pangs' (pieces of cotton cloth, oblong in shape and worn as shawls or scarves); also of ivory. At a distance, the surf looked small from his ship, but the pilot said "Bye and bye, Massa, you can see he be no so little!" The men set off, paddling with a brisk stroke and making a peculiar noise with their lips, 'Whiss, whiss, whiss...'. He now saw a lofted ridge of raging waves. The canoe shot up onto the wave crests and down into the troughs. The men then relaxed and took the canoe up onto the shore with the force of the wave. Many small sharks gathered in the course of this passage, so ravenous that they came close to the paddles. 'Awaiting like live sepulchres to entomb us on their gaping jaws'. The canoe shot onto the sandy beach, and 'we leaped out onto the land; the canoe men manoeuvred the canoe round a point into the still waters of the river mouth, and we embarked again onto still water'. In two hours they were at the wharf in Lagos. An official interpreter was waiting and told George that he must be immediately conducted to the king.

8. Sketch Map of Sierra Leone where George Pilkington served from 1816 onwards, showing the site of Freetown. Freed slaves were settled there from 1787-1792 and called 'creoles'. It served as the capital of British West Africa from 1808-1874.

The author spent three days sweltering on a troop ship in the harbour there in 1942, and it is not surprising that Charlotte Pilkington's two brothers died there in 1816-1820 and she herself was very ill, considering the climate, primitive sanitary conditions and medicines against fevers that must have existed there at the time.

9. The earliest immigrant freed slaves arriving at Sierra Leone, 1787.

10. Freetown in the 19th Century.

11. Fort Victoria, 100 m SW of Cape Coast Castle. A.W. Lawrence (1963) states that Phipps Tower was built in 1702, went in to disrepair and was destroyed by an earthquake in 1796. Pilkington says that he helped in the design of a Martello Tower in 1820-1, and that it was 'Phipps Tower'!. In fact, Fort Victoria clearly resembles a Martello Tower, but it was built in 1837 on the site of Phipps Tower, according to Lawrence. Another, smaller tower was built in 1820, Smiths Tower, later renamed Fort William, and still in existence, but it was square and very small. Pilkington was involved in the design of a Martello Tower, as he states, but it seems that it was not constructed until 1837, on the Phipps Tower site. Another, remote possibility is that a Martello Tower was constructed on the Phipps site in 1820-1, and Fort Victoria was a rebuild in 1837. Whatever the truth, George was clearly involved in the design of one of the Martello Towers there, and it was used as a look-out outpost against Ashantee incursion, which did occur after his brief stay there.

18

12. Cape Coast Castle; the Portuguese called the cape Cabo Corso, which the English corrupted to 'Cape Coast' (A.W. Lawrence 1963). A Swedish fort was built here in 1655, but changed hands several times prior to 1664, when a combined Dutch and English force captured it: it remained in English possession until Ghanaian independence in the 20th Century. It became the headquarters of the British Africa Company, and later the London Committee of Merchants. It had a prolonged and shameful history as a base for export of slaves to America: it had large underground ventilated prisons which could hold 1000 slaves. The slaves were taken out through tunnels under the guns. There were 96 cannon there in 1796. The slave trade was abolished by Britain in 1807, well before George Pilkington visited it. The Crown took it over from the London Committee in 1821, under Governor M'Carthy and a garrison was housed there to repel threatened Ashantee invasion. The guns were by then obsolete and the fortifications needed refurbishment. Royalty and the clergy had no compunction in being involved in the earlier shameful activities of Cape Coast Castle and according to Simon Winchester the slaves were branded 'DY' for Duke of York!

5. Further experiences in West Africa

The palace was reached by passing through the town of Lagos with the attendant: it was enclosed by a huge mud wall, the portal being lofty and decorated with grotesque figures; the 'idol gods of the country'. The gate was opened to their knocking and the interior revealed as a series of squares, surrounded by corridors of galleries, from which doors led to various apartments. They passed through three squares in line, and more squares were revealed on either side. The palace clearly covered an immense area. In the centre of the third square arose the throne, crimson in hue and covered with cowrie shells, which in this part of Africa were used as currency. The royal seat was revealed as a bank of earth coloured with annatto; within it was placed a small canoe manned by grotesque figures, each furnished with a paddle - marine deities?

Three loud reports attracted his attention, due to the interpreter greeting the king, snapping his fingers in a salute, while kneeling with his forehead touching the ground. The king was six foot or more in height and very stout, with a glossy jet-black upper body set off by a large red coral chain reaching to his waist. All he wore was a silk kilt and sandals. He moved to the throne and placed a chair for George. The interpreter remained on his knees!

After a long silence, a young woman, one of the king's 300 wives or attendants, entered by a door opposite the throne, slipped her back to the wall, and sidled around the angle of the wall, finally kneeling before the king. He gave her a bunch of keys and she brought a liquor case, which the king opened, breaking the silence for the first time.

"Sir, will you drink gin, brandy, noyeau or wine?" The king gave the girl a bumper of George's choice, and eyeing that she did not spill a drop, took a glass himself, handing it down to George. When

George had drunk, he locked the case and dismissed his wife, saying:

"What do you want in my country?'
"Gold dust, ivory and cotton pangs," George replied.
"Why not slaves?"
"Because I'm an Englishman."
"Why do not Englishmen buy slaves?"
"They do not think it right that black men should be bought and sold like beasts."

Hearing this, the king laughed contemptuously.

"If they do not think it right themselves, why do they interfere with other nations?"
"Because they possess power and influence as a nation."
"How far is it from hence to England?"
"Six weeks sail by sea."
"What a great water that must be! How far is it to the West Indies?"
"Six weeks sail also."
"By the same water? O what great water! Could you not buy slaves off me, and take them over that water without King George knowing anything about the matter?"

George replied that it might be done, but asked the king what he would do if he discovered any of your subjects disobeying his commands. The king turned the conversation saying "Well, come to me in the morning, and I will sell you plenty of ivory and gold dust."

George asked for permission to purchase fowls, as he had had nothing to eat, but the king said that he would send supper and told the interpreter to guide him to his sleeping quarters. This was a square apartment with high walls, a gallery on one side being the only opening to the air. In the corner was a bed, the head and one side of which was a mud wall, the other side and foot being of basket-work; there was a door for entry. This was presumably a device to keep off mosquitos. The chair and table in the room were covered in dust, so the room had not been used for a long time.

James, his servant, endeavoured to clean up and placed a single candle on the table to lighten the gloom.

"Well", he said, indignantly: "If ever I see massa in a place like dis before! He be dirty, dirty place for true massa!

A jet black man clothed in white now appeared, carrying a tray on his head; removal of the white cloth revealed a delicious looking fish. Before George could accept it, the cook put out his tongue, with the intention of licking it, head to tail. George seized the cook to prevent the execution of his fell design.

The interpreter said;

"Pray, massa, let he lick de fish."
"Oh, no!"
"If you do not, he no leave de fish."
"Why so?"
"Cause, massa, if you go dead will kill he, suppose he no licken."
"Oh, no: I know it is not poisoned."
"No! No! Massa, cook won't trust for a dat, for you can get sick in de night; maybe you catch cold – you die. Den king ask me if cook lick de fish. Suppose I say no, den king cut cook's head off!"

George vainly hoped that the other side would be free from licking, but the cook licked both sides, so George scraped the skin off after the cook had departed and made the best meal of it that he could, before entering his bed through the basket-door, while James slept on the table.

He waited on the king the next morning and was conducted by him through storehouses of ivory, great quantities of firelocks, dollars, cowries, and merchandise of various descriptions, showing off his great comparative wealth. While they were so engaged, the butcher and cook came in, the cook taking charge of the quarter of mutton delivered by the butcher and going through the familiar licking procedure. The king watched seriously to see that every crevice was visited, while the cook showed anxiety as if his life depended on it. The same ceremony was, reportedly, repeated by the cook on serving the dish. This suspicious process was related to the tyranny of the odious traffic in slaves. The monarch, rather than protecting his subjects, betrayed them to the agony of expatriation and servitude more terrible than death. The system recoiled on the king, who was slave to his own fears, living in perpetual dread of poison or assassination.

George presented the king with gifts usual to these occasions and the king gave the townsfolk permission to trade with him by ringing a gong; an immense circle of copper upon a huge pole, carried to prescribed places and struck repeatedly with a long stick. The people were thereby introduced to the new trader.

He stayed there for three weeks, there being only two market days per week, for the convenience of those proceeding to the interior for slaves or merchandise. In fact, the traders brought him very little, because there were two slave ships from Cuba in the river, bringing greater and easier gain to the native traders than the produce which he required. He decided to quit the place, which would have repaid him amply for his risk and expense but for the prevalence of the odious traffic in human flesh.

It was painful to him to see the emissaries of the slave dealers sally forth, with the price of treachery and murder to purchase these

23

unhappy beings, who at the signal of a whoop of war were surprised and torn from peaceful hearths, or yielded their lives in desperate defence. They were compelled to leave their wives and children unprotected to the brutal and savage mercies of their conquerors. From such sorties, he had seen them brought in to factories, where they were examined as a groom would inspect a horse; their price being determined by soundness and condition, childhood, youth, age and the like. Once value was fixed, they were chained together until numbers were sufficient for embarkation, which generally took place within about two hours, to avoid the cruisers.

He remarked that Christian professors to whom all war was unlawful, taught the uninstructed Africans to fight saying "How are we to protect our possessions without war", when they themselves had caused the conflicts with the native people by their unchristian actions, in engaging in the slave trade. He wrote about this after his later conversion to Christian beliefs while in Trinidad, but it is quite apparent that he was a man who from the very start of his career, in the West Indies, respected the rights of his fellow men, whatever their race or colour.

Leaving Lagos through the surf of the bar, he observed on the sea-shore many whitened bones of those who in the hurry of embarkation had been wrested by the billows from their mercenary possessors, and had been dashed back on the beach, in preferable lifelessness.

He sailed for Princes Island, a Portuguese settlement, and remained there some weeks disposing of the remainder of his cargo, and purposing to return at once to Sierra Leone. However, a British Ship arrived in distress, and was sold by the authorities at the request of the Captain. Here there was little competition, and he purchased a cargo of palm oil at one penny a gallon, to be delivered on board his or another vessel, free of all other charges.

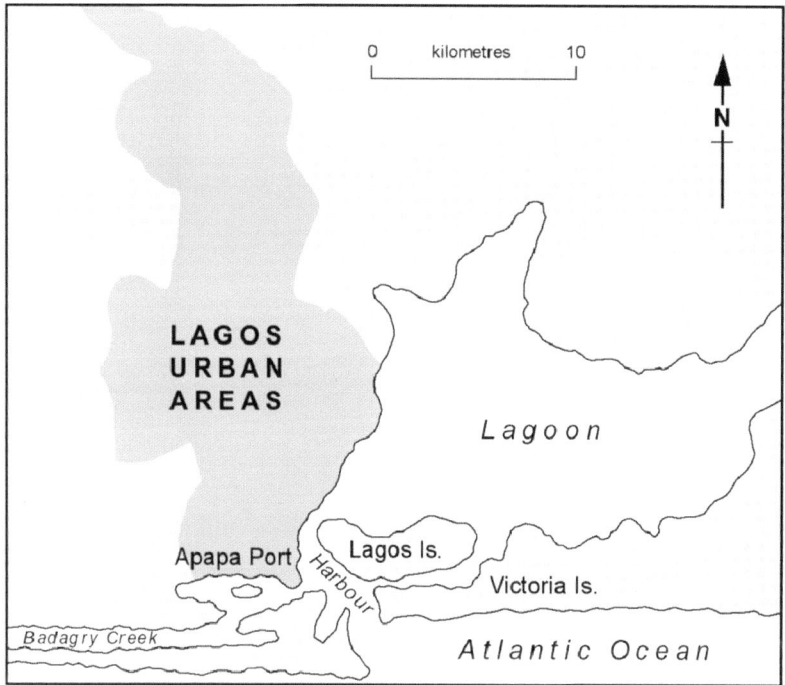

13. Lagos was a Yoruba settlement of Awori people, initially called Oko. The explorer Rui de Sequeira visited it in 1472, naming the area Lago de Curamo (Lago means lakes in Portuguese). From 1404 onwards it was the main slave trade centre of the Yoruba Kings. In 1841, twenty years after George Pilkington's visit, King Oba Akitoye tried to ban the slave trade, but the merchants resisted and installed his brother. The British supported the deposed brother and he was reinstalled in 1851 as the Oba of Lagos. The British annexed the colony in 1861, crushing the slave trade and controlling the palm and other trades.

14. Principe Island, where George Pilkington, stayed after leaving Lagos, was a Portuguese possession, with San Tomé. It is equatorial and tropical, and was the site of plantations, but then became a stopping off point for ships involved in the slave trade. Slavery was abolished by the Portuguese in 1876, but forced labour is reported to have continued. This illustration shows ancient Portuguese buildings at St Antonio on the island.

6. Disaster strikes at Cape Lopez

George calculated that he would clear £10,000, as the oil could fetch 8 shillings a gallon in Brazil. So he wrote to his wife in Sierra Leone telling her to embrace the first chance of joining him in Brazil, so that he might be spared the crossing back to fetch her: then he would go direct to England with her.

The governor of the isle (now called Principe) begged him to take his secretary with him, for he was desirous of sending some despatches to the Emperor. George declined passage money, but good provisions and wine were sent on board.

We do know that he had a captain for his ship, because he was no mariner; and the captain was probably someone used to coasting voyages in small ships. The ship was clearly very small and suitable for coasting, not braving the Atlantic crossing. The embarkation of the secretary was accompanied by a number of officials and friends sending him off. After setting sail, he spent his time either talking to the very courtly secretary or musing on the financial gain from his cargo, a happy re-union with his wife, and return to England with the purchase of a cottage.

Alas, after three days, the ship ran onto a sandbank in sight Cape Lopez, in what is now Gabon, 15 miles south of the Equator. The captain was probably sailing south to pick up favourable winds for the Atlantic crossing. They endeavoured in vain to get her off by putting out anchors and hauling on them, but she had struck at high tide and at low tide turned on her side.

The secretary appeared to be dreadfully alarmed and, as a boat came from the land, was determined to go ashore rather than spend another night aboard. George remonstrated with him, saying that he did not know what he was going to, but he called for his trunks and departed. The next morning at least 50 canoes approached, the first one bearing the King of Cape Lopez, who enquired whether they wanted help. George replied in the affirmative, saying that he would pay for it. The king then came aboard, and finding it impossible to float the vessel off the sand bank, declared it a wreck and commenced to plunder the cargo. After he and 'his black myrmidons' had achieved some progress in the plunder, he directed George to go ashore, whereupon he embarked in the royal boat accompanied by his captain. The other boats took off his crew, while his majesty and the residue industriously continued to plunder his property. As the boat pushed off, he saw the copper bottom above the water and a tear dropped from his eye, considering his now blighted prospects. However, this was not his first reverse he had met with in life, so he summoned all the fortitude that he could muster and had ceased to sigh over the ruin by the time the boat reached the shore.

The blacks landed and left them, apparently consulting their fetish deity as to their fate. In an hour they returned and required the two foremost crewmen to give up their cutlasses. On seeing this, the captain declared that he would fight for his life. George told him that it was useless for twelve men to resist such a large mob, but the captain said "O, I will not be killed like a sheep: I will die like a man!" This, he was assured, would not ensure his own safety and would cause the destruction of others. The natives came to their boat and desired George to hand them his weapon, which he did without hesitation. They then commanded the captain to do likewise, and he did so, with much angry violence. The king's canoes then came up and they were separated, one white man to each boat.

The captain, thinking that he would be killed, cried "farewell, the fault is yours!" George was moved to the king's canoe, which then made its way up the creek to the town. He concluded that any refusal to give up their weapons would have cost them their lives.

He acknowledged that his restraint was not out of Christian motives, but dictated by the expediency of the moment.

On arrival at the town, 300 women belonging to the king came down to the wharf, each carrying a portion of the spoils. They led the procession to the palace, a large well-built house two and a half storeys high with a framework of wood and galleries all round: the walls were neatly constructed of reeds. A comfortable bed was prepared for him in a back gallery, and he procured something for supper, after being informed that half the lately-seized cargo remained his property and he was at liberty to purchase what he pleased. He went to sleep in a slightly lighter heart!

In the morning, as he descended from the gallery, the secretary passed below; George was glad to see him, but he rushed past without his usual formal greeting, only giving a condescending bow. He was, in fact, hurrying to the king, before whom his trunks lay opened. The king was about to claim his right of 'wrecum maris', which in olden times had been exercised by Lords of the Manor in England, living close to the sea. He was dividing up the contents according to this right.

Separating the shirts, the king said 'This is for you, that for me.'

Next came a blue military coat, thickly embroidered with silvery lace.

'This is for me,' said the king.
'I only have one,' answered the secretary.
'I am sorry for that: if you had another I would give it to you!' said the king.

Next came a cocked hat, a silver scabbard and a sword belt.

'These are for me!" said the king.

Thus he appropriated every single article to himself, allowing the secretary one if there were two.

At the bottom of the trunk were bags containing dollars.

'What are these?'
'The Emperor's money.'

His majesty at first let the secretary keep all the money, for brass and iron were the only valuable metals in his eye. However, later he gave up his share, but only for the value in cloth of three slaves, which must have been a considerable sum.

This being paid, the court closed, and the people with all duty carried the secretary's share to his lodgings. Surprisingly, he had now regained some of his composure and offered George his customary greeting; 'Pardon monsieur, sans cérémonie!' George concluded that he had in fact been treated most unceremoniously!

On the next day, George was at the court and standing beside a native man who was engaged in discourse with the king. He noticed one of the king's warriors stealing along behind them, approaching them ready to spring. He was not without some trepidation, and dared not look round. However, his justifiable anxiety was allayed when the warrior seized his neighbour, pinioning him by his elbows. The king now spoke angrily to the captive, stating in the native language the cause of his detention. He was destined to be sold as a slave. The poor man made no resistance, and scarcely remonstrated, knowing that it was useless. George concluded that the warrior desired to show the king how dexterous he was in kidnapping natives from the villages.

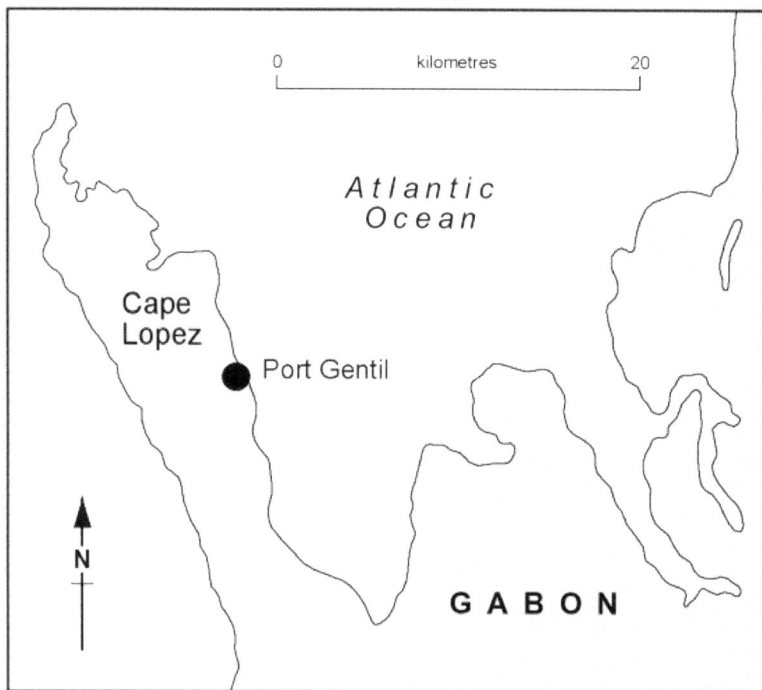

15. The modern city of Port Gentil, Gabon, is off Cape Lopez, where George Pilkington was wrecked. It was the kingdom of Orungu when George was held captive there, and this was at that time centred on Cape Lopez, where there was a metal working and boat building culture. Initially they used slaves internally, and were purchasers rather than exporters, buying them with ivory, but later developed an export trade, though the transatlantic exportation was minor compared with neighbouring kingdoms (~5000 per year in 1788), and by the mid-19th Century, when the Mpongwe nearby were not selling their own people, they tended to export as slaves their own felons and trouble makers. In 1853 King Ombango-Rogombe agreed to abandon the slave trade, but it continued secretly upriver until the 1870's. When George Pilkington was wrecked there in 1821, the trade was flourishing, but it is clear from his account that the King then also picked on felons in his own tribe and exported them to America.

7. Escape on a slave ship

George Pilkington remained on this coast for seven weeks, fitting out his boat as the only way to expedite his departure. His ship had a captain with him, and the king concluded, as George afterwards discovered, that he was a very great man with plenty of ships, and the king desired him to attract him to revisit the place with merchandise. The people there, like all along this coast, wished to attract European merchandise to their shores.   For such merchandise they would even murder, steal and sell each other. The king, a pagan, spoke several European languages, proving his many dealings with mercantile nations.   He had 300 wives or servants, who wore a distinctive number of brass rings, each varying in size with the shape of the leg. These made a noise like the clashing of a chain with every step, and on their approach all men had to turn away their faces, on the pain of being tied up and thrown in the river! One time George saw all 300 assembled before the king, who affirmed their number.   When George remarked that it was the same number as possessed by the King of Lagos, the king said "What! Then, I will have 50 more: no man shall have as many wives as the King of Cape Lopez!"

Meanwhile, George had made progress with fitting out the ship's boat, which had been recovered from the wreck.   When ready for sea, he embarked for Prince's Island, about 200 miles distant. The 12 men crew were close-packed, with provisions and water casks, but 'had little fear of the enterprise'. However, they had no caboose (a cooking stove), so on meeting a vessel asked for a half-barrel, which with some sand in it could serve as such very well.

On hearing that they were bound for Prince's Island, the captain of this vessel said;

"You'll never perform that voyage in such a boat. I must beg of you to come aboard my ship. I will land you safely at St.Thomas's Island in six weeks. As a Christian I cannot allow you to proceed in so miserable a boat."

This offer was readily embraced, but on reaching the deck George realised at once that it was a slave ship! He told the captain that as a British subject he could not continue on board. The captain strenuously insisted that as a Christian man he could not let him expose himself and his crew to such imminent peril, and George eventually consented. The captain treated him with great hospitality, and during the voyage endeavoured to reconcile his Christian principles with taking two hundred and fifty men, women and children from their families and country to sell them to perpetual slavery, and rescuing twelve men for the purpose of speeding them to their families and country! Expediency, George remarked, will be the rule observed by many professors of religion.

In this Spanish ship, the slaves were stowed away like packages, the men having no more space than allowed them to lie down, with an iron rod passed through manacles on their ankles: thus they could only sit up or extend themselves in a recumbent position. The women were kept separate under the captain and officers' cabin. They were allowed the privilege of being brought on deck to dance every evening before sunset. This exercise was conducted by the boatswain with a 'cat' in his hand. Those that laboured were reminded with a stroke of the 'cat', that their 'friend present' and not their absent relatives required all their consideration. The slaves were fed on boiled pease or beans, and received just the attention and no more that would be given to a cargo of horses.

George was pleased to find his friend the Portuguese secretary on board. They reached the island of Saint Thomas at the appointed time, and he hired a lodging for himself and the crew on the first floor of a large house, for five shillings a month. Provisions were proportionally cheap. He sold his coral, the only merchandise left from the wreck, for £150, after paying all his expenses while on the island.

The Governor came on a visit to this part of his delegated domain from Prince's Island, and regretted George's misfortune, paying him every civility. The custom was for the island's inhabitants to entertain the Governor for three days, and thus George received daily visits from his orderly sergeant, inviting him to dinner, where he found an assemblage of people of all colours – black, white and brown colonels of the militia; black and white priests; black and white civilians; all waiting in an anteroom. The Governor was very old and because of failing eyesight always had a servant behind him, touching his pigtail dexterously to guide him without observation. The Governor sat at the head of the table, the Lieutenant Governor and other officers at the foot. They had to carve successive dishes, which was done with large sabre-like knives. The flesh was cut out wherever it could be excavated, in shapeless masses, which 'would beggar even Crabbe's description'. These were passed down the table, right and left, in a 'voyage of discovery'. A dish of cabbage reached George some time before any meat solicited his attention. There was no regard for the taste or preference of the guests. Here, the favourite exclamation of his Portuguese friend, the secretary, seemed appropriate – sans cérémonie! The guests just had to wait for their preferred dish to the time when it was brought under the sabre-knife.

The first course was an entire bullock, less horns and hooves. An immense dish of salt pork, yams and sweet potatoes was put in the centre of the table. A course of mutton and a large porker with two small ones, roasted whole, took up station at the head and foot of the table, like a mother attending her farrow. This was followed by poultry, pastry and preserves, washed down with palatable wines.

Coffee was produced and then the aged Governor filled a bumper and toasted the company, expressing the desire that they all would live for many years. He then rose from the table, and was steered away by his pilot.

During his time at St Thomas Island, George had been occupied at preparing his boat with a half-deck for the purpose of beating to Sierra Leone, a distance of more than 1500 miles. The boat had presumably been transported on board the Spanish Slave Ship to the Island. However, providentially, a British Man-of War arrived, they were well received on board, and arrived at Sierra Leone after six weeks voyage. There, to his great distress, George found that his wife had already followed his instructions and set sail for Brazil.

Having but £150 in his pocket, he resolved to sail for England, but again providentially, after his wife's ship had visited Goree, Senegal, and the English Settlement on the Gambia River, in passing again southwards it had run short of water, and called in to replenish it at Sierra Leone. Thus, 'to their mutual surprise and joy', they were reunited and all the incidents, danger and penurian loss were put aside.

16. San Tomé is the larger of the two former Portuguese Islands and is equatorial and tropical. These islands, which are volcanic and extend the line of volcanoes in the Cameroons seaward, were reportedly uninhabited when the Portuguese discovered them in 1470, though this is difficult to believe. Like Principe, it became a stopping off point for slave ships. These islands now form an independent state, one of the smallest in Africa, but with hydrocarbon potential. The view shows a cathedral on San Tomé, dating from the Portuguese colonial era, well described by George Pilkington, who stayed there after rescue by a slave ship.

17. The La Rochelle slave ship 'Le Saphir' in 1741, source 'La Traite Rochelaise', origins anonymous 18th C.

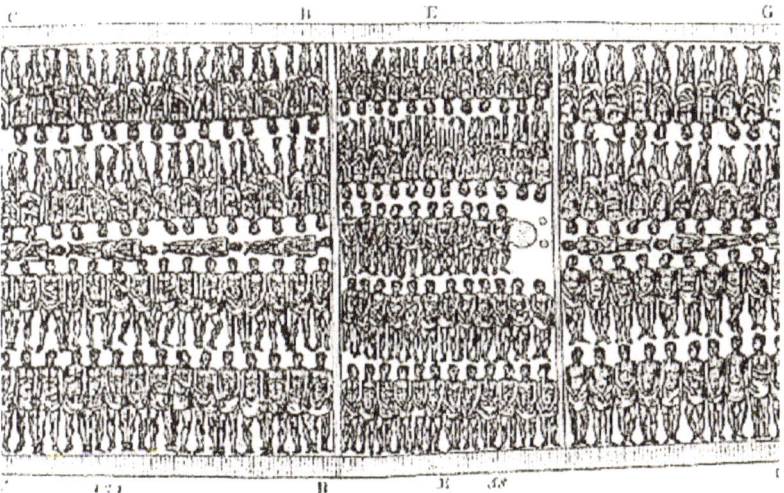

18. Diagram showing the way the slaves were packed into the slave ships, in irons.

8. Back to the West Indies

After some weeks stay in the colony where they had long been domesticated (from 1817-1821), and 'to which they felt some attachment despite the seasons of sickness and sorrow experienced there', they took passage on a frigate which was sailing to England via the West Indies, and after twenty-two days passage fetched up in Barbados. The Captain was a religious man and held prayer for the entire crew every Sunday. The naval discipline was strict and one day a week was assigned to punishment of any offenders, who would be paraded before the captain and told of their faults, then given the chance to make their own case. Most of them were told; "take off your shirt, sir", and they were lashed to the gratings by the companion way by the boatswain's mate, who with his muscular arm administered as many strokes of the 'cat' as the Captain ordained. George remarks that he had at that time to learn that this expediency was at variance with Gospel principles.

They sailed on from Barbados to Antigua where he had served in the Royal Engineers, and thence to Trinidad where they landed in October 1821.

Trinidad was under the governorship of Sir Ralph Jones Woodford (1784-1828), who had come to the colony in 1813, recently taken over from the Spanish. Port of Spain had been destroyed by fire in 1806 and Sir Ralph was instigating reconstruction programmes. George became Civil Engineer and Surveyor General under him, and may well have been involved in setting out the streets such as Woodford Square, Queens Park Savannah, the Botanic Gardens: and also in the Protestant and Catholic Cathedrals.

In Trinidad, George found thus his professional services much in request, whether commercially or governmentally. The 'door of the

World's riches' appeared to open once more for him'. He laboured assiduously in his profession in a private capacity and was shortly appointed to the Quartermaster General's department of the Colonial Governor, with the rank of Captain; the rank he had formerly held in the Royal Engineers. This appointment involved him in heavy expenses as he had to keep a charger and purchase an extravagantly embroidered uniform; and he also lost much valuable time in attending balls and 'routes', while no emolument was attached to the situation. He admitted that at the time he was 'attempting to stride over his neighbour, attempting the great game of business'. He remarked that some men elevate themselves to become separated from their fellow men by a kind of golden fence, and seem to require a special law for their protection – the law of honour by which they seem to be entitled to fight duels. At this time he was a professed Deist – a term, the definition of which is confused, but during the eighteenth and early nineteenth centuries it was used to denote those against formal religion.

It formed part of his duty to attend with the Governor all military reviews and occasions, and on January 1st 1825, four years after landing in Trinidad, he went in procession to a Roman Catholic chapel; this attendance was under the terms of the capitulation made at the conquest of the colony in 1798, by which Spanish laws and customs were to be respected. The Governor, on this occasion, was representing the Spanish King, and sat on a dais near the altar, while George sat in an aisle. The streets were lined with a gazing multitude and a salute by artillery greeted the Governor on his approach. The prayers were said in a low tone and in Latin, but then a Catholic Bishop said in English "In the name of God" and preached on the text:

"When the Son of Man cometh, shall he find faith on Earth?"

The preacher set out to prove the divinity of Jesus Christ. George smiled secretly at first, thinking of his favourite objection as a Deist; 'Why does not the Almighty send a miracle in the present day, to set aside the unbelief of the multitude?' Surprisingly, though, his heart responded to the appeal: 'The power and authority must be divine' he thought. Then he thought 'behold, the very miracle!' He wrote that he received conviction at this time, but had yet to learn the more blessed effects of conversion.

He returned to Arima where he then resided, about 16 miles from Port of Spain, the Capital. When his wife Charlotte took her books to her closet to pray, as usual, he asked if she would take him in to pray with her, to her delight.

Some day later he argued the case for his new Christian belief with a brother Deist, who said 'You tell me that you are now a Christian: three weeks ago you were a Deist. But you were always a man who acted uprightly: persons do not complain of any vile conduct by you; you were charitable; and even did acts which Christians boast of but never perform. You offered your life for a friend; what change do you find in your heart to lift you above that estate?'

George adds a footnote here. This friend alluded to George Pilkington having offered to fight a duel on behalf of a friend, so circumstanced that he could not fight himself, in order that he might obtain redress for some grievances. George was baffled by this questioning, and could not at the time offer an answer. He made small progress in his new belief for two years, being concerned with worldly affairs at Arima, where there was no chapel, only a Roman Catholic Church.

During this two-year interval, George recollected some slight indications of improvement. In the village of Arima there was a magistrate, a great favourite of the Governor, which made him excessively proud and overbearing. He had a quarrel with George, though he treated him outwardly with civility. George tried to become less and less opposed to him, though the magistrate was unaware of this. At length the Governor did something that offended the magistrate and he resigned in a huff. His resignation was unexpectedly accepted and thereby he lost part of his income. Shortly after this his cocoa estate became valueless and finally the money, which he obtained as half-pay ceased to be paid. His acquaintances then forsook him, because of his tyrannical behaviour while in office. George, practising the principle of return of good for evil, took him, his wife and his five children under his roof.

The Governor, hearing this was astonished and at once cultivated a more intimate relationship with George, and in March 1828, offered him a civil situation at £800 per annum, provided he gave up his private work. George accepted the offer. He had to move to Port of Spain, the capital, and now could attend divine service. George attributed the change in his circumstances to the hand of God, but considered himself unworthy, considering the sins of his youth (which he did not specify).

On September 22nd 1828, he was appointed to command a corps of light cavalry with the rank of Major, and on 24th of September was confirmed in his appointment as town surveyor. He had been acting as such. He was now obliged to attend parades every Sunday, and at the time he did not consider this was unlawful in the light of his Christian beliefs, though he did write to the Governor asking to be relieved of this obligation on the first Sunday of each month, when communion was celebrated. The Governor, however, made no concession to this request. George did from now on observe closet meditation and searching of his heart from now on, at a particular hour on each day.

George found that he had the habit of 'unconscious swearing' and determined the next time that he swore to go on a diet of bread and water. However, though he fasted from Monday to Friday, on being told that a portion of the public works had been spoiled by inefficiency, uttered an impatient exclamation. His wife 'looked as if she had received a shot'. He determined to fast for another week, despite her remonstrances, and in this he succeeded. Since then he had never sworn.

He then came to believe that his Christian beliefs meant that he should oppose the prejudices in which he lived. The King, in council, had directed that the free coloured people should have equal rights with the white people, civil or military. He was therefore determined to appoint a black person as cadet; the first stage leading to appointment as a cornet. The officers in his unit agreed with this unanimously.

He then waited on the Governor, General Grant (the original Governor, Woodford, must have been replaced: he died at about this time) and acquainted him of his intent. His Excellency admitted that it would be a great point gained, but requested him not to do so: 'For, he said, I shall have the whole community on my back!'. George asked what answer he should give to Mr Le Blanc, the person in question. 'Do what you please,' was the answer, 'but on no account send me the recommendation before the next parade'. The Governor was then away in the 'Spanish Main', being absent for about three months. George decided, because of his conscience, to appoint Mr Le Blanc, subject to the Governor's approval and confirmation, a step which the Colonel of another corps had taken in the case of two white men. Timidity, he believed would have been a crime against his beliefs.

The Governor had obviously washed his hands of responsibility like Pontius Pilate, and it is clear that George was tactless, though principled, and was risking his family, now a wife and three children's (including my great grandmother, Clara's) future: his years in Trinidad had been the longest period of 'calm seas' in his life. This action brought the end to this calm period and the termination of his service in Trinidad

George was never one to blame others for his misfortunes, and admits that it was entirely his responsibility, not General Grant's. He followed his conscience and the order of the government at home.

I shall put the account of what happened in his own words:

"If I had applied a match to the powder magazine of the Citadel, I could not have created a greater sensation in the Colony. On the procedure of the Colonel who had appointed two white officers, I heard no comment whatever, whilst mine incited the indignant opposition of the Governor, of the whites, more especially those who were connected with the government. The result to my private prospects was sufficiently disastrous. The coloured people, finding that they could not obtain commissions elsewhere, flocked to my standard; and, as this was likely to end in the entire dissolution of one of the other corps, I was made victim to the political expediency of the moment, and on the 10th of June, 1830, received directions to confine myself to my staff duties as Quartermaster General, and the command of the corps was given to another. Just at the same juncture, also, my situation as town surveyor was found to be burdensome to the public (although the fees for surveys executed, formed the principal portion of the salary), and the office was suppressed. To conclude this singular coincidence, my situation as colonial engineer, which I had undertaken for £800 per annum, under an engagement to give up my private profession, was now reduced to £300 sterling: a sum altogether inadequate to support my family in this expensive Colony: and as now, I had no friends among the white inhabitants, I could not possibly engage in the private practice of my profession. I therefore came to the resolution of embarking for England, in order to obtain (which I never for a moment imagined I could fail to procure) an order from the Colonial Secretary for the balance of salary, amounting to £1146.18s, which was justly due to me, but which the Trinidad government refused to pay me".

"As soon as it was generally known that I was about to leave the island, I received an address signed by four hundred of the coloured inhabitants, a copy of which I shall affix to my narrative, as an interesting proof of the gratitude they manifest for the slightest benefit conferred on them. I had now closed my affairs, and with only £90 in my purse, after paying my passage, I embarked for England on 22nd November 1830. Never shall I forget the extreme attention of the coloured people on this occasion; although ignorant of the state of my finances, they heaped on board the usual store, and comforts of all kinds for the passage, whilst those who attended the embarkation of myself and family, cheered us with loud acclamations, till their voices could be heard no longer in the wind."

The address is reproduced below:-

ADDRESS
Of the coloured people of African descent to George Pilkington, Esq, on his departure from the Colony of Trinidad, 20th July, 1830.
"When the suffering Sons of Africa discover an individual among their white fellow-subjects in this Colony, whose philanthropy leads him openly and fearlessly to favour the moral and political advancement of an oppressed and degraded race of men; whose soul, soaring above the influence of narrow-minded policy, selfishness, and the

long cherished prejudices of his white brethren, rejects the principles of their system, as warring against the will of Providence: When they behold that genuine British subject, who from practical conviction, and a due sense of obedience to the mandates of a gracious King, and in furtherance of the views of the wise Councils of his Government, laying aside all personal interest, and disregarding the frowns and displeasure of men, conscientiously stand foremost against the conflict of local opinions and the pressure of combination: When they see this true Patriot aiding and encouraging the great work of charity - the amelioration of his species – to which the finger of the Almighty manifestly points all true lovers of Christianity: We say, Sir, when such rare and novel characteristics appear in a white Colonist of this hemisphere, gratitude on their part to that individual, as well as justice to human virtues, demand a mark of admiration as distinguishing the phenomenon as extraordinary.

In you, Sir, we have found all those virtues, to us truly estimable. We bear testimony that in your public conduct and character, as an officer commanding a military corps of cavalry, and holding office at will of the Municipal Corporation, you disinterestedly and frankly afforded to applicants of colour in your corps, every fair opportunity of preferment to militia rank to which the King has graciously pleased to admit them. You were the only commanding officer who dared to lead this example of breaking the barrier of prejudice: and who, displaying a high sense of public justice, ventured to dissent from a system of combination adopted to prevent the access of coloured people to military honours in the Island of Trinidad. The result of your temerity is on record, in the Colonial proceedings of the day. We would not shock the world, or insult the judgment of good men, by a detail of the injury and persecution you have suffered on that account. As a gentleman and father of an infant family, we most deeply and keenly feel the sacrifices you have

45

endured; your case is indeed a lamentable instance of the tremendous influence wielded by the white oligarchy in this Colony, ruthless in its effects, when directed to crush, even it own members, if found dissentient or converts. The rectitude of your motives, and the solaces of an approving conscience, are rewards above the gift of men. The cause you have espoused, you need not be ashamed of. We address you therefore, as a true and genuine friend, and on behalf of a class of your fellow subjects, who respect and admire your noble patriotism and exalted merit. We beg leave to present to you this feeble testimony of their gratitude, and the offering of hearts unfeignedly thankful, duly sensible of that friendship and sympathy which you have on all occasions manifested, particularly in our late endeavours to obtain from the whites of this Colony, a reasonable acquiescence in the late orders of the King in our favour.

We beg your acceptance of our sincere wishes for your health, prosperity, and happiness through life, and with the greatest pleasure we subscribe ourselves your very faithful friends, and loyal subjects."

Signed by 400 Persons among whom were 24 Proprietors of Plantations.

....

They also gave him a letter to the same effect, which is printed in Appendix to his 1836 book.

George seems to have been extremely unlucky, in getting mixed up between the benevolent policies of Governor Woodford (who was apparently trying to follow King George's precepts and who died in 1828) and Governor Grant, who succeeded him and would have nothing of it, correctly fearing the English settler's wrath. With King William IV on the throne the precepts lapsed; and the colour prejudices, particularly strong among the British and Americans, survived for many decades.

....

19. Columbus named the island of Trinidad on July 31 1498 for the Holy Trinity. The native Amerindians were called 'Caribs' and used as slaves on other islands. The Spanish made raids early on to obtain slaves, but did not colonise until 1530, when Antonio Sedeño was granted a contract to settle and control the slave trade. Spanish rule, nominally dating from 1498, ended with surrender to a British Fleet in 1797, and the slave trade was abolished in 1807, though there was much circumvention of this decree afterwards. As in Russia, after Alexander II, the Czar Liberator, there was a problem (totally unforeseen in Russia) of what to do with the liberated slaves. In Trinidad, after the 1807 abolition, they were termed 'apprentices', and still tied to employers. Full emancipation was not finally legalised until 1838, after George Pilkington's time there. It has been discovered that George Pilkington employed such former slaves ('apprentices'). No doubt he did: he obviously had to accept the system realistically because he needed labour. This was in his early years in Trinidad and he was not then as is wrongly stated 'an itinerant preacher', indeed this was prior to his Pauline conversion! Several hundred black slaves, from the US South who had been recruited in the Royal Marines, were granted land there in 1816. It is clear that there was trouble with the 'coloured' population throughout George Pilkington's years there, in the 1820's, mostly in the enlightened Governor Woodford's time (he died in 1828). The picture shows Port of Spain, the capital, in the 19th Century. Arima, where George lived most of his years in Trinidad, was the home of the Amerindians, and Governor Woodford determined to preserve Spanish laws and customs, and protected the Amerindians: journeying yearly to their feast at the mission there of Santa Rosa.

48

9. Friendless in England

The vessel made a prosperous voyage of seven weeks sailing, but arriving in the Channel, was driven into Falmouth by a storm, which damaged it and necessitated repairs. His wife had a relative at Bideford, so he left her there, imminently expecting his fourth child, with the three infants, and proceeded himself to London to seek the money owed to him by the Trinidad government. They arrived at Bideford on 12th January, 1831. Three days later he proceeded to London and he addressed a letter on the 9th of February to the Governor of Trinidad, who was then in London, requesting him to place his claim before the Secretary of State. He anxiously awaited a reply for 18 days without avail, and so called at the Governor's residence. The latter was not in and so George decided to write his name and address on a blank card: being shown into the study he saw his 'unfortunate letter' unopened on the Governor's desk. The next day he received an answer declining to forward his claim. He therefore wrote directly to the Secretary of State, who, after a delay, also replied, declining to acknowledge his claim.

He now had no friend or relative to call on for help, having been 26 years overseas. All his kindred were either dead or dispersed overseas in the military or naval professions. He was not only consuming his limited funds, but was harassed by the widow of a deceased friend, who called at his lodging and calumnied him, together with an 'enemy', as a dishonest and immoral man, for which charge there was no substance at all. The repetition of this annoyance caused him to change his lodgings, and, according to his Christian principles, he prayed for them, rather than bringing an action for libel.

At breakfast, on 10th August 1831, the day after that on which he received the final letter from the letter from the Secretary of State, his landlady entered his parlour and required him to discharge his account of £2.10s on the following day, as she needed the money to pay the tax collector. He had but a single shilling in his pocket. However, he promised so to do, remembering that he had some articles in his trunks that he could pawn for cash; but as she reached the stairway he heard a boy's voice enquiring whether he was at home. On receiving an affirmative reply, he said 'Give him this'. On opening it he found only a £5 note with the words 'Accept this trifle with the best wishes of a kind-hearted friend, whose prayers attend you!' His bosom 'filled with gratitude at this gift from an unknown donor', he paid the landlady and remitted £2 to his wife, only keeping 10s for himself.

About this time a friend presented him with a book "the Principles of Christian Religion" in which he read that the military service which he had previously engaged in was unlawful for Christians, and this so impressed him that he held this view for the rest of his life. It is to the year 1831 that this conviction, which guided much of his itinerant 'preaching' and 'lecturing', must be attributed.

George, at this juncture, thought himself 'completely tumbled in the dust', but worse was to come. Now with his purse entirely empty he had to dispose of his embroidered coat and military trappings. He believed that his tribulation was God's punishment for his past transgressions. His few shillings retained out of the £5 were soon reduced to a half-penny, which he resolved not to part with, since it would procure nothing useful. He did visit the Anti-Slavery Office and there was invited by the friendly clerks to tea with them, which temporarily answered his purpose for the moment. He visited them more than once! Then on August 26th 1831, the postman delivered an order for £50 in order to pay some trifling expenses incurred attending their charter by a Masonic Lodge that he had been instrumental and establishing (it seems likely that this was overseas), and he was told to accept the balance as a small tribute of their esteem (this may have been an oblique way of showing their charity). From this he retained more than £40, a not inconsiderable sum in those times, but this was 'barely sufficient for the exigencies of his family'.

Through this crisis time, attacks on his character by the enemies aforementioned recommenced, they circulating most injurious reports. The woman thought of the money he was supposed to owe her, whilst the other believed that his actions in the West Indies had destroyed his worldly interests there. This suggests that his actions had made him a pariah even in England, among some people with interests in the West Indies, and had probably caused unrest among the coloured people who worked on Plantations there.

We know that George even petitioned the King, now William IV in place of George IV. The Governor, Colonial Secretary and even possibly the King, understandably if pusillanimously, 'kept their heads below the parapet', until the unrest in Trinidad settled with time.

It is of interest that the Governor and Secretary of State even saw fit to ignore George IV's instructions, because they did not want to bring the wrath of the whites on their heads. George had acted through the best of motives, but was a man before his time. Even when I was in the East African colonies in the 1940's and 1950's I believe that a similar situation could have arisen, but there appeared to be a tacit agreement not to do anything that would arouse the same of the white farmers, particularly those of South African origin in the Eldoret area, brought up on apartheid.

George was separated from his wife and children (the youngest of whom, born on 27th of January 1831, 15 days after arrival in

England, he had not seen for at least a year: my researches reveal that this was his second daughter, Augusta). He presumably did not visit Bideford because he had no money and everything available he sent to his wife, except for small amounts for his upkeep. He led a hand to mouth existence. He 'felt like a sparrow on the rooftops', without any prospect of relief.

On leaving Trinidad, he had said to his wife, in order to cheer her spirits: "Charlotte, whilst I have this head and this right hand, neither you nor the children shall suffer need." He concluded that the Almighty was punishing him for this boast, and was showing him that his vaunt was unavailing. His wife too, during this hard time, had apparently regarded this vaunt with secret suspicion. George had so often fallen and recovered in his career, that he was blinded by false hopes.

At Bideford, his wife's relative was taken ill and died on 17th August 1831. Also, one of the two trustees, for money held in trust for her, had died and the other refused to let her have the interest on this money (this appears to our eyes to be illegal, but the rights of women at that time were negligible, it was then 'a Man's world'). She became very ill and this prevented her from even arguing legally for her rights. She required close attention night and day throughout this illness. Between them they were obliged to part with everything they owned, to pay the heavy expenses that devolved on to them. Even so she was left with debts amounting to £45 and as the calls were urgent: she wrote George a touching letter on 6th December 1831, which too evidently portrayed to him that they were 'struggling through deep waters' and that 'nothing but the divine hand could be their succour'.

"I would be happy on bread and water for the rest of my life, if united with you and your children, nor would I care how hard I worked to make your home comfortable. Sometimes, when the clouds of adversity are darkest and most impenetrable, relief is at hand. Would that it might prove so! Oh that you were with me that we might pray together – strengthen each other – stimulate each other to love God more and more – to serve him with never dying fervour! But these are his gifts, which he has engaged to bestow on those who seek him by faith on the name, merit and righteousness, and all sufficiency of his Son. We are not straitened in Him, let us not be straitened in ourselves: let us remember that the Saviour loves large petitions; we cannot ask too much. Oh, how greatly we stand in need of spiritual strength! How much we require to be driven out of ourselves, and to look with longing eyes, ever, ever, ever, unto Jesus."

George had attended for the three months the one Edward Irving's chapel, but when he found that three or four of his congregation were under the delusion that they spoke in strange tongues, which neither they themselves or others could understand, he left, believing them to be under delusion. He includes an 18 page appendix on this practice in his 1836 book. In communicating his reasons for rejecting this practice to some Christian friends, he was requested to publish his views for the good of the community: so he prepared a small pamphlet which was with the publisher when he received his wife's call of distress. He was thus able to reply to his wife that the 'book' had attracted extraordinary demand, day by day, and cash was paid as the books were delivered. At the end of the four weeks, he was able to send her the £45, after which there was no more demand!

He now had only a few shillings himself, but on 28th December 1831 (he writes 1832, but this is a mistake, because in a later chapter he writes from Hammersmith in mid-1832) he was invited by a stranger, impressed by his pamphlet, to stay with him at his home. There were tribulations to come, but it seems that at this point he achieved some turn round in his fortunes.

10. An abortive decision to emigrate to New South Wales

On 17th February 1832, George received a letter from his wife stating that she needed £8 to pay her rent: the money was due on Wednesday evening that week. He hoped to receive a loan from Trinidad, and had formulated the idea of emigrating with his family to New South Wales. Meanwhile, he had but one shilling in his pocket!

He had so far been disappointed in receiving the loan from Trinidad, though he had some reason to believe that it would be granted. Knowing that a West Indies packet was due, with that faint hope he walked to the offices of J.W. in Aldermanbury and of E.G. in Mark Lane. On his way he made a resolution to even seek a labourer's job in his profession, though at that time even labourer's jobs were hard to come by, being the subject of great competition. He even considered the lowest such job of all, a crossing-sweeper (as so eloquently described by Dickens in Bleak House), but wryly supposed that there was even competition for that and a need for experience of crossings! In this gloomy mood, his mood was brightened when seeing the text "Seek ye first the Kingdom of God and his righteousness: and all things shall be added unto you".

Arriving at J.W.'s counting house, and having before a slight introduction to him, and therefore being able to have letters addressed through him, he stated the cause of his leaving the West Indies. There was no letter, but J.W. remarked that Lord C. was about to be reinstated and others restored to the Service, so it might be fruitful for him to seek redress of the King. George replied that this he had done with no avail, and he added that he had no intention of returning to Military Service, because he now believed that it was unchristian to bear arms. J.W. said that he did not entirely agree with this view, though he admired the principle, but he referred him to a pamphlet by Lieutenant Thrush, who had left naval service on the same ground. He would obtain it from St. Paul's if George came back later that day. George agreed, and proceeded to E.G.'s counting house with no avail.

When he returned, J.W. handed him the pamphlet. George thanked him and was just leaving when J.W. stopped him and said: "Excuse me, I think you are in distress!" and handed him a £5 note. George burst into tears of gratitude. The kindness of this benefactor did not end here. George told him that he had come to England to obtain an order from the Secretary of State, on the Colonial Government for the balance of his salary due to him, and that he intended to migrate to New South Wales and work there in his profession, as he had done in Trinidad. J.W. proposed that he should raise the money by subscription among his friends, but George assured him that there was no-one on whom he could make such a call. J.W. then said that he would himself put in £50 at the head of the list and further, give him £20 to purchase the necessary instruments (theodolite etc.). George mentioned one or two possible contributors and agreed to try this out, more to please the generous J.W., than with any confidence.

J.W., on the next day, proposed that George should go himself and leave his family behind, but George's heart 'sickened at this idea'. Reluctantly, though he started to write to his wife about such a plan, for he knew she had experienced a long period of sorrow during their months of separation, and that her health was very delicate due to her exposure to tropical climates. But as he wrote, he realised that even to pay his passage and settle outstanding debts in Bideford, he would need much more money.

A day or two later he received the following letter:-

"My dear Sir: it has occurred to me, that on making the application to the gentlemen you mentioned, in town and probably your family connections also, it would be better not to speak of your separation from your wife and family, and going alone to New Holland, but that the aid sought was for the expenses for the voyage for all, and which, under a favourable arrangement, might be reduced to one hundred and fifty pounds. My nephew hopes that the charge may not be to the ship, more than a hundred and twenty pounds; but several incidental expenses would in all likelihood amount to an additional thirty pounds. As, probably, your personal application would admit more ample explanation, and be more judicious, I must beg of you, in order to meet the lurking prejudices of the world, to use the enclosed notes.... (three notes to tradesmen to give him what he required for his personal accoutrement), ...and reassume your external appearance of your rank in life. I feel assured that you will rightly appreciate my motive in asking this, and if the West India money comes, we can consider this merely as an anticipation of a portion of it. I would thank you to let me know what other instruments than a theodolite you may require, as it is possible that some of my friends may have them to spare, or may point out the most economical mode of obtaining them. I am, my dear Sir, very truly yours, J.W."

George had obviously come to be very down at the heel in his dress and appearance due to prolonged poverty. He returned to Hammersmith, not very optimistic, but penned a more cheerful letter to his wife. He found that he now had to leave his abode there, because of change in his host's circumstances, and, after thanking his host's wife (his host was away), he departed thence on 4th March 1832 with but a shilling in his pocket, and found a bed a lodging house. The next day J.W. gave him £10, especially for his wife. He had now found that £220 would be required to cover emigration of the family, and raised his contribution to £100, telling George to go to work obtaining the remainder. George realised that he had little chance of raising the money, and suggested Canada instead, which would be cheaper, but J.W. would not hear of this and offered him £200, and gave him £5 for his current expenses, which allowed him to obtain a lodging close to the London Docks, where he started preparations for embarkation.

On the 7th of March he found a vessel going to New South Wales, and wrote cheerfully to his wife, seeing the end to his troubles. Having made arrangements for sailing and picking up his wife at Plymouth, disaster struck; after some weeks waiting for embarkation: on the 16th of May, the Captain of the ship informed him that they could not call at Plymouth on account of cholera breaking out there. Then J.W. suffered a pecuniary loss, which made it impossible for him to advance the entire sum: he could only advance the £60 already expended. Whilst, shortly afterwards the ship did receive health clearance to call at Plymouth, J.W. came to the conclusion that the 'Great Disposer of all events' had decreed that he should be given an opportunity of retracting his offer and they both agreed that it was the will of God that George and his family should not proceed to that part of the world.

George now dreaded telling his wife of the ill turn of events. It is clear that, he had improved his dress and appearance, for, he of all people was now the target of beggars! It is probable that this improvement in his appearance, very soon put him on the upward path in his affairs. It is apparent from his words that J.W. was most generous man, and really helped him and his wife over the nadir in their fortunes.

....

11. Association with the Anti-Slavery Society

It was probably a good thing that George Pilkington did not succeed in emigrating with his family to Australia: he was now 47 years old and his own health may well have been affected by his service in hot climates and months of deprivation in London. To have made such a new start with a wife and four young children would have taxed a much younger man, let alone the long sea voyage.

George deferred telling his wife about the cancellation of these plans until 6th July 1832, when time and circumstances rendered it imperative. He merely informed her that the agreement with the captain of that particular ship was annulled because of the captain's inability to call in at Plymouth. His wife apparently replied with a poem consisting of three line verses expressing her belief in him, a poem which is printed in his book of 1836.

George now, perhaps because of his improved appearance, obtained some work with his friend, J.R. at Hammersmith, 'posting his books', which were very much in arrears, and he also obtained board and lodging with him.

Meanwhile, J.W. on June 11th 1832, wrote that he had contacted the coloured people in Trinidad, for whose interests George had suffered much persecution, but unfortunately the reply was negative. He concluded: "from my heart, I truly commiserate with your accumulate disappointments and most sincerely regret that my hands fall powerless before the requisitions of my feelings; the privilege would be joyful to me in the one case as the other, but it is withheld. In the need there will be light – the arm that afflicts is a father's arm. It is indeed, in such a moment, truly humbling to designate myself, your impotent friend J.W".

It is clear from this that J.W. shared George's strong belief that one's life was ruled by providence and that the almighty sent blessings and afflictions. George replied that he was in no way cast down and that J.W. had already done more for him than he could, or ought, to have expected, and that he was consoled by his sympathy.

He was still finding it difficult to tell his wife of the collapse of his plans for emigration, but on receiving a reply from her complaining that he had not replied to her previous letter, he had, on July 23rd 1832 to write again, excusing himself by saying that he had nothing to report. He also mentioned that her suit in Chancery (the dilatory court described in Bleak House) against her cousin's trustee would necessitate her giving evidence in person, and the court might pay her expenses in coming to London: or if not some Christian friends would pay them if the court declined.

He told her that the coloured people in Trinidad could not help him, and that J.W. was distressed beyond measure. He told her of his work on J.R.'s books which prevented him from being penniless. He also mentioned a visit to the Anti-Slavery Society, where J.C. gave him an excellent dinner and also gave him some work to do, which obliged him to take a Hansom cab home, which he reached with 2s 10d in his pocket (this work was almost certainly circulating pamphlets for them, and the cab was required because he had to carry the leaflets).

Finally he added that he had spent some time on the day before praying for her and the children.

Having been engaged by the Anti-Slavery Society to collect subscriptions, George now moved to George Street, Euston Square, where he rented a single room for 4s 6d per week, and he was now able to send a greater part of £3 per week to support his family.

Ever generous, he at this time helped a converted Jew, whom he had befriended at Hammersmith, and who, on August 16th 1832 came to his door and said "I have been living like a dog for the past week". He gave him small amounts of money for some time. One day he walked to Holborn with the Jew, and on parting told him that he had 4s 6d in his pocket, but was assured that God would provide more. In the city he called on J.W., and as he entered the office the latter said: "You are the very person I desired to see. The West India packet has arrived and the coloured inhabitants of Trinidad have directed me to pay you £100 sterling."

He presented George with their letter:

> 'Sir, We are directed by the committee of the coloured inhabitants of this island to place the sum of £100 at your disposal, and to request acceptance thereof through the hands of J.W.Esq. They have learned with unfeigned regret, the painful embarrassments in which you are placed, and sincerely sympathise with your misfortunes. They would willingly have increased the sum now tendered to you, but the necessity they are under of making new and extraordinary efforts for the attainment of their rights, which require considerable pecuniary means, and the almost incredible state of general distress which exists in the colony, render it impossible for them to offer you a sum more appreciative of the great esteem which they entertain for you. Sincerely wishing yourself and family a change of fortune, and future health and happiness, we have the honour to remain Sir, your very obedient and humble servants: Lewis Lebre Jun., Joseph C. Lebre."

This was the last direction from which George Pilkington was expecting pecuniary help, for their previous communication to J.W. had stated that all their funds were going towards attainment of their civil rights, and he felt that this cause outweighed his own distress, but he was gratified by the esteem in which they held him, and believed that their action confirmed the universal love that God the father extends to all men of one flesh, irrespective of colour.

After receiving £10 from J.W. he left, intending to return to J.W. on the next morning when his mind was more settled. On reaching home, he penned a brief letter to his wife, and spent the evening in meditation and prayer.

On the next morning J.W. asked what he intended to do now. George replied that he would settle the debts at Bideford and bring his family to London. J.W. was surprised by this and said that with this increased funding he might still reach Canada and find an opening there for his professional skills. He was alarmed at George's resolution saying; "Remember that I have done all that I can. If you are again reduced to the last farthing, there is no resource for you in this country." However, George, to satisfy him, replied that he would leave the decision to his wife.

It is quite clear from the following pages in his book, that the idea of emigrating to Canada stayed with George and Charlotte for some time, but it would have required considerable further funding, and never came to fruition.

....

12. Re-united with wife & children after 21 month separation

George Pilkington sent his wife enough money for a land carriage from Bideford to Plymouth and thence by steam-boat to London; also sufficient to pay her debts. He mentioned J.W.'s proposal that they should issue promissory notes to their creditors and appropriate George's very limited fund to conveying the family to Canada. He added his views on the subject, and left the decision regarding emigration to her, praying for the Lord's guidance in this matter. It is unclear what her views concerning emigration were, but this proposal was not yet abandoned. In the event, she slightly overran the funds sent in settling her debts, but not being willing to delay her departure, made arrangements for George to meet her on arrival of the steam-boat in London to pay the fare. In parting with her friends, she was particularly sad at leaving Grace Clark, who, though aged only 27, had been bedridden for four years with a crippling ailment. She arranged to stay with a friend on the last evening in Bideford, and this lady pressed £5 in her hands saying; "Excuse the liberty, but I cannot feel easy without entreating you to accept this, as I have reason to believe that it will be required before you reach your destination." Charlotte was much struck by this generosity, but assured her that she had made arrangements with George to meet her with the fare money; she would need no more money and she declined the offer. However, the lady was so pressing that she accepted it. This was indeed fortunate, for on arriving at Plymouth accompanied by her four children, she found that the fare had to be paid before embarkation.

On hearing of this, George quoted a text from Psalm 34 in thankfulness to the generosity of this sister-in-Christ: "He shall give his angels charge over thee. They shall keep thee in all thy ways. They shall bear thee up in their hands, lest thou dash thy foot against a stone" (the subject of one of the most beautiful choruses in Mendelssohn's 'Elijah', of which I have sung the tenor part).

Meanwhile George had taken a house on an agreement that he could give three months notice to quit. He does not say where in London, but my detective work suggests that it was in Islington (20 Barnesbury Street). He wrote that being an old soldier, he had learnt to manage without superfluities. He purchased essential articles only, a few cooking utensils, a fender and fire irons; a chair, cup and saucer, knife and fork for each member of the family; blankets and mattresses which were laid on the floor of the bedrooms. Their trunks formed a Turkish settee round the otherwise empty parlour. He found that his friend, the Jew, was most useful in purchasing second-hand articles at a very low rate.

He took possession of the house on Friday September 7th 1833, laid in a bushel of coals and two large loaves of bread, as well as a small portion of tea and sugar, and sent a joint to the bakers on Saturday, hoping that the family would arrive by steam-boat on the Sabbath, and they all could feast together on the day set aside for public worship. However, the boat did not arrive until Monday 10th of September, when he was at last reunited with Charlotte and his babes, the youngest twenty months old whom he had not seen, and the four-year old – by my calculation, his second son, Woodford - scarcely recognised him! He concluded that 'the furnace through which they had lately passed had removed much of the dross of their fallen nature, and rendered them new creatures.' Here we are seeing a strong belief in 'original sin' and that our sufferings are given to us by the almighty to rectify our faults!

They soon reached the house: the amount he possessed in the world amounted to £25, plus his small items of furniture, etc. He handed the money to Charlotte as 'Commissary-in-Chief'. Despite, the still precarious state of their finances, they were both confident as to the future. They were, despite their poverty, now pursued by the neighbouring bakers and milkmen for their custom!

Now he sought employment in every direction, and eventually heard that the Temperance Society required a lecturer. He was directed to approach one R.B., who had some influence with the committee. Though their funds were low, the latter asked him to attend him on the next Saturday at the Anti-Slavery Society's office. R.B. was sitting in committee, and after a wait the secretary, J.C., emerged, saying 'R.B. is fighting a hard battle for you: he desires you to be appointed Lecturer'. Half an hour later he was informed that he was appointed such, at a salary of £200 per annum (exclusive of expenses). George took £5 on account and ran to the omnibus, for 'his legs could not carry him home quick enough'.

He travelled for the Society for some months, and delivered some eighty or ninety lectures at public meetings on the subject of Slavery. Of course, he understood his subject well, having seen this iniquitous trade from the source in West Africa and the slave ship, and the product in the West Indies, first hand. This engagement came to an end in March 1833, when the Government Ministry, unable to resist the pressure of current public opinion, made Slavery a Government concern. So now George had to look again for employment.

....

13. More lecturing with and without sponsors

George frittered away much time in an unremitting search for permanent employment after March 1833, and decided also to do something on his own, which he believed was 'following the leadings of the Lord'. His wife agreed with this new approach and he also started delivering tracts and visiting the sick. He did this until 21st May 1833, when he attended the annual meeting of the Peace Society. He was there asked to move a resolution and expressed his feelings about the unlawfulness of War. Three weeks later he delivered a public lecture at Islington on the subject, making no collection, as he felt that 'the Lord would recompense him when he thought it necessary'.

He once again at this time became conscious that he was prone to anger at the various ill practices rife in Society and 'asked the Lord to grant him the power of the spirit to subdue his evil propensity towards anger'. He recollected his experience of trying to subdue anger and swearing in the West Indies, and once again abstained from eating and drinking anything for thirty-six hours. This self-imposed fasting could have threatened his health, though there is no evidence of any ill health until 1838 in his writings.

Unfortunately, soon after his fast, one of his small daughters intruded on an earnest conversation, and he uttered a word of annoyance. So he repeated the self-imposed fasting regime.

He quotes a hymn by Charles Wesley which he found appropriate at that time:

"All things are possible to him,
That can in Jesu's name believe;
Lord I no more thy truth blaspheme,
Thy truth I lovingly receive.
I can, I do believe in thee,
All things are possible to me"

"The most impossible of all,
Is that I e'er from sin should cease;
Yet shall it be - I know it shall;
Jesus, look to thy faithfulness.
If nothing is too hard for thee,
All things are possible to me."

"When thou the work of faith has wrought,
I here shall in thine image shine;
Nor sin is dead, or word, or thought:
Let men exclaim, and fiends repine,
They cannot break the firm decree,
All things are possible to me."

He remained without employment until 8th July 1833, when he was sitting in his parlour and heard the baker come to the door, asking how many loaves they wanted. He had a sudden conviction that he ought not to order bread when he had no money to pay for it. He feared to tell his wife of this, so he went out, praying to God for assistance, and called at several places hoping to hear something profitable about employment, but to no avail. On his return he met his wife, with a cheerful countenance, and she told him that there was a letter, from one C.B of C--------r.

She stated that any influence that she may have possessed would be insufficient to procure him an official situation, but, on reading the sentences expressed by him at the Annual General Meeting, she had commissioned B. of London to present him with £10, desiring that his name be not mentioned. He thus discharged his small accounts, including the house rent, with pleasure, and remembered 'this condescension of his Heavenly Father' every time he heard the crash of the baker's basket at the door.

Shortly after this several sums were received, amounting to nearly £20: these were intended as part of a subscription raised with the intention of transporting him and his family to Canada, but the amount raised was far short of what was required for the purpose, so this attempt to emigrate proved abortive and George concluded that England was the field that 'he believed the Lord had destined that he should labour for a time, in a manner that he knew not then.'

His funds once again became exhausted, but at the end of October 1833 he received a visit from J.S., a brother lecturer for the Anti-Slavery Society, who had searched out his abode with difficulty, travelling 15 miles on foot. He drew George's attention to a situation that had been offered to himself, but did not wish to take up. He suggested that George accompany him to the Labourers' Friend Society, by whom George was now engaged as an agent and lecturer. He made sure, before signing up, that he could still, when opportunity offered in his spare time, continue lecturing on Peace and Temperance, provided that this did not interfere with his duties as their agent. The salary offered was very small and was barely sufficient to support his family, with the utmost frugality.

He travelled sometime in this employment, holding one public meeting in a garden and allotment at Ipswich, where he lectured on the great advantage which accrued by letting small pieces of land to labourers. He lectured at several other towns before reaching Norwich, where local arrangements prevented him holding meetings for the Society, but he collected subscriptions and donations, staying for 3 weeks. He gave a lecture on peace and this attracted a great attendance, and resulted in the formation of a Peace Society in that city.

Returning to London, he found that he still needed £20 to procure clothes for the children and other necessary expenses. They resolved to 'live lower still'. He stayed for 10 or 12 days at Guildford and on the last evening lectured on the principle of peace. Here, he received a sum of £20, forwarded from Norwich by someone who had shown a great interest in the principle of peace, and he attributed the fact that this was the exact sum that he needed at the time, again to the workings of Providence.

Obtaining a place here for the delivery of his lecture on peace, he had a far from smooth ride. One man said that it was impossible to love one's neighbour as oneself, and left the meeting! Another, a chapel minister, gave George as sort of catechism on his knowledge of doctrine. George replied that all he knew was the gospel, and 'that he would go upstairs, step by step'. The minister then said 'but who will lift your legs up?". George regarded this as a puerile question, but he does not appear to have fully understood the meaning.

At church service here, George rebuked a couple of fashionably-dressed men in the pew in front for repeatedly conversing 'as in a drawing room', during the prayers. When they continued he said 'This is not decent.' 'What?' was the reply: ''You are here to pray.' The older man stopped the younger continuing to chat, but gave George a furious look. George 'expected to be horsewhipped', but on leaving nothing ensued! In telling this story, he shows a flash of humour.

Continuing to Brighton, he stayed there three weeks and gave one lecture for the Labourer's Friend Society, and two on peace. However, on his return to London, the Society objected to him lecturing on peace and delivering tracts on that subject, even though it was done in his spare time. He attended the Committee, and assured them that he was neither employed by the Peace or the Temperance Society, but lectured on the subjects on his own volition. He was asked if he urged Christians not to enlist. This he said he did and ever would do. The answer he received was "You will alienate our friends: this is an insuperable objection!" He replied, "but yet you know it is the truth!" The speaker was a 'minister of the Gospel of Peace', George noted, and a General present did not offer a word. 'The soldier was in the rear, the minister in the forefront of the battle!' George was given two or three days to decide, but did not give in, and was mindful to quit, the Society's payroll, especially as the salary was so small: this he did.

He now feared to be 'cast again into the furnace', but still hoped that the Peace Society might employ him, overriding their objection to him urging listeners not to enlist (it is clear that these two societies were closely connected). However, on the 7th March 1834, they informed him that they did not have the funds to employ him in an official capacity. The Chairman of the Committee presented him with £5, which he said he would accept because necessity required it. He was now without sponsors.

George was now 'on the billows again', but his faith 'remained unshaken. On March 8th he met J.S., one of his fellow lecturers for the Anti Slavery Society, at breakfast with R.B. He told them that he was 'under a cloud as never before'. J.S. was desirous of establishing a branch of the Temperance Society at the west end of the town and, as he had introduced George to the Labourers' Friend Society, they called in there on their way, and George finally resigned his post with them. At four o'clock, he met R.B. again, who asked him "How is the cloud?". George replied "As yet I see nothing clearly'. R.B. told him that he had been requested by someone who had attended his 6th June meeting in Islington, where he had made no collection, to present him with £10. George took this to be an indication of divine approval of his conduct, and 'heard a voice, as from a cloud tell him; "Preach peace!".' When his mind awoke from his reverie, he found the 'cloud disappeared' and 'he saw and followed a pillar of fire'.

He thus decided to continue lecturing on his own volition, without a sponsor. In a chapel at Whetstone, in a very isolated spot, he was surprised to attract 350 people. At Mile End, the attendance was about 600, and at Jewin Street, about 1000. However, returning to Hammersmith, where he had friends, they objected to his lecturing, because 'a defensive war was a Christian duty.' George quotes at length from the Old Testament to prove that it was not so! At Richmond on April 2nd, he again met with objection, his bills advertising the lecture, being obliterated by further bills cancelling the meeting. The deacon, who had encouraged him to come, offered to pay his expenses, but he declined to accept the money to show his sincerity.

Finding it difficult to get the use of chapels in London and its suburbs, George determined to attempt a long route, though his means were nearly exhausted. Not sure in what direction to go, he received a favourable communication from two strangers whom he had met on the top of a coach, returning from Richmond on 28th of March. He therefore decided to go in a westwards direction. He left the city with only 35s in his pocket to preach 'peace and goodwill'.

At Uxbridge, the independent Minister received him civilly, but declined to lend him his chapel because of the great disturbance caused by a Peace Meeting 12 months previously. He recommended him to borrow the school room. George made all the arrangements and posted the bills. He was invited to tea at a house, where he met the secretary of the Temperance Society, who lamented the fact that some of his speakers failed to turn up. George offered to lecture on Temperance, but was told "You have come to this town to lecture on a most unpopular subject, and, as it is the nature of man to identify the person with his subject, so I feel persuaded that your advocacy would be injurious to our cause: besides which we are not so badly off as to require your help."

However, George's lecture on peace was generally received with acclamation, though there a few dissentients. One man was overheard saying that he would like to strike George to see if he would bear it patiently. However, a person listening said "The fool should know that your practice could not cancel out the precept of the Lord". George made no collection, but said that anyone wanting to contribute to the cost of the proceedings could send the money to his hotel that night. Two people put 5s in his hand and the Independent Minister said "You have declared the truth tonight" and put 10s in his hand. Another gave him half a crown, invited him to supper, and gave him a further £4.15s there.

This was the first lecture in a series in which George travelled 840 miles in two months, terminating at home in early May 1834. He returned home twice during that period, spending only a night there, but at the end had three weeks at home, only lecturing once at Wandsworth. He travelled on foot, by coach and even in a carrier's cart. He visited some places more than once, securing a suitable venue and posting bills advertising his lectures on the first visit (for example to Bristol and Bath). He appears to have been tireless, for example at Bath, talking to 200 children and a teacher in the morning for one hour, to 400 children in the afternoon for another hour and the next evening addressing 500 people.

To recount the details as he did in his 1836 book, which terminates at the end of this set of lectures in May 1834, would be tedious, so I have tabulated the details of this 'progress'.

Table 1: Towns visited on first extensive tour April- May 1834

Town	No attended	Remarks
Whetstone	350	
Mile End	600	
Jewin Street	1000	
Uxbridge	600	
High Wycombe		No attendance given
Henley	250	
Marlow		No attendance given, chapel full to overflowing Service in afternoon here for 'lower classes only!'
Reading	1500	A minister refused the use of chapel, calling George a traitor and a liar
Newbury	750	
Devizes	700	
Melksham	700	
Calne	300	
Bath	200+400+500	
Bristol	500	
Thornbury	500	Piece of music dedicated to him
Cirencester	600	

Fairford	150	Want of notice
Faringdon	300	

On his return, his wife told him that a benefactor had ordered him a new hat. His wife had told him to purchase a new one on his last visit, but he had refused. She had obviously devised a ploy to circumvent his obstinacy. She was clearly a strong character - this emerges from a picture of her in 1856-7, when living in South Africa, and visiting her daughter Clara (my great-grandmother) and her large family in Blackheath - but more of that later.

....

14. Marathon lecturer on peace, slavery & temperance

George Pilkington ends his 1836 book, "The Doctrine of Particular Providence" with a summary of his self-motivated and unsponsored lectures on peace and temperance, over much of England. However there is a problem in that this actually covers his itinerary well after the closure of his description of his initial itinerary to the west of England, the last chronicled in the first book. Thus, I have reproduced the essentials of that summary in a later Chapter, after covering all his missionary journeys in the British Isles up to his last, in Ireland in 1838.

The second book "Travels through the United Kingdom: In the Cause of Peace on Earth" is more 'lumpen' than the first which covers his life up to the age of 49: the second covers only 4 years from 1834-1838, from the age of 49-53. It consists of three parts, after a brief recapitulation in Introduction: seven chapters cover his six lecturing itineraries up to early July 1835, when he was called on to rescue 'Edwin' from confinement on an Island in the Shetland. He occupied three months on this venture, and it is recounted in no less than 10 chapters of the second book. Then he returns to his lecturing, which occupied him from October 1835 to the first of March 1838: Seven chapters (XIV-XX) are occupied with details of these later nine itineraries in England and three more (XXI-XXIII) to with his single itinerary in Ireland and return to his old home in Dublin. He ends quite inconsequentially with the story of how he helped an Irish Catholic wife and child to rejoin the soldier father in Gibraltar. The only further writing by him, other than engineering-related documents, is a plea to Brazil in 1841 to abandon slavery (their rejoinder is also held in the British Library). I do know something of his later life, which came as a great surprise, but this is only gathered in by a detective exercise from other peoples writings, including my mother, Dorothy McCall's, two reminiscences.

The contents of the second book are unsuitable for very detailed reproduction and I have adopted the method of tabulating his itineraries: in the text I have brought out the more interesting incidences during his journeys, recounted the extraordinary affair of 'Edwin', summarised his final overview in the first book, then given my own appreciation of George to 1841, when he was active opposing slavery in Brazil. He apparently travelled there for two years. I have then added chapter on what is known of his life from 1841, when he was 56 years old, to 1857, when, at the age of 72, we have the last record of him. We know that he emigrated to South Africa in 1848 and died in South Africa, at the age of 73, in 1858.

I prepared a full set of tabulations of his itineraries during his period as an itinerant lecturer on peace, slavery and temperance. The full set is contained in an archive which consists of the full unedited text, a full set of 41 illustrations. In this edited version of my text, I have limited the tables to four of his itineraries (his original trial itinerary to western England, two of his later itineraries to northern and eastern England and his itinerary in Ireland. I have summarised all his itineraries in a fifth table.

15. The next seven itineraries

During his itineraries, George mentioned many interesting incidents, problems and antagonism, and also the many admirable people that he encountered. His first itinerary out to the west was relatively free from antagonism. He mentions a strange incident at Gloucester, where a young man of 28, the secretary to the Friends had been sent to meet him. It is clear that at this time the Quakers and Independents worked in quite close collaboration. This man had been blind for nine years but directed George skilfully, moving surprisingly fast along the street. George asked how he could work as secretary, but he said he could do it quite well with an amanuensis helping him. Of course there was no Braille in those days. George considered that this was a shining example to the many 'professors of Christianity' who find excuses for idleness.

He convinced a half-pay colonel at Gloucester of the correctness of his arguments about opposing even a defensive war, and advocating overcoming evil with good. A Captain also expressed the view that 'we have been engaged in a very sinful profession'. At Droitwich, the landlord refused payment for his lodging: this was not an infrequent happening during his many subsequent travels.

In his second Itinerary he encountered vigorous opposition at Tamworth, from a lawyer, a wholesale tea dealer and classical tutor. This was supported by clapping from the audience and cries of 'infidels!', 'infidels!'. These opponents published a virulent pamphlet against him three days later, and were incensed when some ladies answered with another pamphlet on his behalf. They thought he was the author of this. They wrote another even more abusive tract, and were astonished to find that their opponents 'were of that sex which seems foremost in the Christian warfare'.

George quotes from the second hostile pamphlet:

"The emissaries of Satan, not infrequently assume the garb of the angels of light; especially when they wish to engage any part of the religious world in their service: I will not assert that the lecturer is one of them, but I fancied that I saw more than once, the cloven foot protrude from under the vestment which was thrown but loosely around". Letter to the inhabitants of Tamworth, page 2.

Strong stuff! It is not clear what aroused such ire, and surely George did not wear any religious vestment; so the last sentence must be metaphorical: they are alluding to the fact that he had no license to preach?

At Birmingham, a Roman Catholic priest later apologised for the behaviour of the people of Tamworth and complimented George on his noble pair of lungs! He had apparently spoken for two hours and then continued the discussion for another hour.

Also at Birmingham, a former acquaintance in Trinidad walked seven miles to hear him and remarked that he was 'like someone raised from the dead', alluding to his conversion from unbelief. A Lieutenant suggested giving up his half pay, being so impressed by George's arguments about peace, but a minister present said that this man was advanced in years, sickly, and had a large family to support, so George took the benevolent view and advised him that there was no need to act now.

On his 3rd Itinerary at Bedford, George lectured in the chapel of the pastor John Bunyan, which made a great impression on him. At Newport Pagnell, a member of the audience wanted him to be more clear about his pecuniary situation (still fragile!), as then more would contribute? However, at Leicester a 'disciple' had said that a plain avowal of his poverty was not consistent with the high spirit of truth of which he wished to bear testimony. George remarked that on this subject, if he listened to the opinions of others, he would be blown about like a weathercock. He felt that 'the Great Shepherd would so regulate men's minds that he would be supplied with the necessary requirements of the day'. At Leek, a small boy put three shillings in his hand! Here also his lodging expenses had been defrayed by a friend, when he came to pay them. However, at Pontefract, he refused money from a wealthy host because the latter did not entirely agree with his arguments about war. Here he lectured to Methodists and members of the Independent Church. He was run two miles in a gig to catch a canal boat, yet another method of travel on his journeys.

At Ackworth, he lectured and was entertained at a school run by the Quakers. The boys were kept on one side and the girls on the other. During the meal the children did not speak a word, using signs only when they wanted to attract the attention of the boy waiters. At dinner with the teachers, the sexes were also segregated. The food was very plain, and all wore the plain dress of the Quakers. The apartments were neat and well aired, and the children slept two to a bed. The behaviour on the playground was also very ordered, and a teacher suggested that a resemblance to military manoeuvres might breed a warlike attitude in the children. George replied that it was a Christian order, in no way military.

George had at this time to swear an affidavit as executor to a relative of his. He had misgivings about the propriety of doing this, perhaps a viewpoint obtained from the Quakers. He accepted the command 'Swear not at all!". He had to find a less scrupulous lawyer, to get round this, and travelled 320 miles to London on this account, cancelling five lectures. At the same time he had to appear in court, and was appalled by the swearwords uttered by the criminals there awaiting trial and the tolerance shown of it by the court. When he declined to swear an Oath, he was asked whether he was a Quaker! He was allowed to 'affirm', and he admits that the court was very keen to get rid of him quickly. He frequently shows such flashes of humour. He was greatly impressed by the Quakers, and later on attended their services.

His 5th Itinerary was interrupted by a Parliamentary election, all his venues being occupied and he returned to London via a coach from Bawtry. He found his nephew by marriage staying with his family. This was George O'Brien, the son of Captain O'Brien of the 38th Regiment, who had married George's wife's sister (Mary?), now deceased. A boy, the only surviving child of the sister, he had been put in a school near London. His father had spent ten years in military service in the east and ten more in the West Indies. George relates how his wife, Charlotte, had a dream in which she saw him in female attire, and resembling her deceased sister: in the dream he said 'Do not neglect me'. Hearing three days later that the father had died, and with Charlotte much distressed, George decided to adopt him, as a fifth child. A friend agreed to pay for his schooling at a school run by one John Willey. George says that he acquitted himself well and repaid their kindness. My mother in her book "When that I was" refers to him as visiting from Argentina later on, and being a 'rolling stone'. She got the facts wrong, something she rarely did, and said that he was no relation, and the product of George Pilkington's bee in his bonnet that everyone should adopt one orphan, let alone adding to one's wife's burdens. In fact, it was Charlotte who took him in and was delighted when George adopted him. He was a blood relation of Clara Rouse, my great grandmother. The story about the dream is strange, and it is not clear how Charlotte managed to find him and take him in. Probably, because of his father's death, he was penniless and he or a guardian approached Charlotte. So now George had five children, and his pecuniary affairs still remained precarious.

He relates little about his 6th Itinerary (Table 2, reproduced as an example), but notes that after ending his lectures with a statement that he was led to do them by faith, but his pecuniary situation was inadequate, he decided not to mention his pecuniary situation at all. At the end of this itinerary he had £120, not a small sum in those days, and even paid £20 towards an unwilling debt that he had incurred to a supporter of the ANTI-HUMAN-RIGHT PARTY in Trinidad (this surely is a name coined by George!), at the troubled end of his time there – he had repaid £45 in all, but £250 remained, which he promised to pay in the future.

His 7th Itinerary, however, taxed his funds, as there were few branch coaches in Lincolnshire and Norfolk, and he had to hire gigs. In one such journey, the gig driver was returning to Lynn, when he was stopped by a woman running out and reporting two men fighting in a field nearby. Trying to stop the fight, both men turned on this short, slender, delicate man. He received a blow in the stomach. The men asked him why he had interfered, and he answered that it was simply a desire to reconcile them (he later told George that he only intervened because he was inspired by George's lecture on peace). The two men desisted and shook hands, and with the woman, thanked him for his act. George visited him when laid up to recover in Lynn, and felt humbled.

Going to Fakenham, he travelled by carrier's wagon and breakfasted at 'a baiting house' on 'a biscuit and half a pint of milk' for which he paid two shillings. Not a very sustaining diet. At Foulsham he lectured in a Baptist chapel and at East Dereham in an Independent Chapel. It is clear that his hosts were almost entirely of Non-Conformist sects.

Table 2: Itinerary 6, an example of one of his itineraries

Town	Summary of details
Hoddesdon	4.2.1835 – 7.3.1835
Halford	1017 miles, 40 towns
Ware	56 lectures on peace in 64 days: to 31,850 persons: 1900 on temperance
Royston	Addresses to 7327 children
Baldock	Parents and teachers 5550
St. Neots	
and on to ↓	*then* ↓
St. Ives	Waterville
Huntingdon	Hartlepool
Earith	Yarm
Chatteris	Stockton
March	Stokesly
Wisbech	Guisborough
Spalding	Whitby
York	Pickering
Thirsk	Helmsley
Northallerton	Kirby Moorside
Darlington	New Malton
Newcastle	Easingwold
North Shields	Scarborough
South Shields	Bridlington
Sunderland	Driffield
Durham	Hull
Hexham	Beverley

16. The "Edwin" rescue interlude

On 3.7.1835, George returned home with £8 in his pocket. Invited to dine with a friend, G., he was informed that the Hon. Edwin ------ --, had been confined as a maniac on Papa Stour, a remote island in the Shetlands, for some 25 years. A lady traveller had lately visited this island and found that he was perfectly sane. In fact, Charlotte had informed George of this three days earlier, but he had concluded that the person who had informed her of this had imposed on her, so incredulous was it that such an outrage could have remained unredressed for so many years in the British Empire. George now asked of his friend, G., "Do you believe it?" G. replied that he did, and then introduced George to the lady, M.W., who was in the next room. She was habited like a Quaker, but professed to be a Methodist. We know now that she was a Miss Catharine Watson.

She told him that she had been engaged in a religious tour of the Shetland Islands, and while on her way to Papa Stour, one of the boatman had remarked that she would meet the ' Mad Mr E." , as some persons called him, though no persons acquainted with him could believe that he was insane. She was invited to stay in 'the only decent house on the island', that of Edwin's 'keeper'. She had several conversations with Edwin, and found him to be 'gentle, intelligent and obliging to all who had intercourse with him'. She noted the moroseness and severity of those around him, and the neglect by his relatives. There were only 25 persons on Papa Stour, and it was difficult for Edwin to escape, for he was penniless; also the 'Lairds' were accustomed to maltreat the populace on these isles if they disregarded their regulations.

A letter had been given to Miss M.W. addressed to her in Edwin's hand. It ended:

'As for myself, I would wish, dear Madam, to get away from the company of the wicked, who make my life a burden, and if there is any possibility in contriving how it may be done, I shall be indebted to you all the days of my life. Dr Clarke seemed to be my friend, for the short time he was here; if by any means I could get to him, he could be the means of letting me have access to some of my friends, by which I might accomplish the thing I much long for. But ambition is far from my prospects. If I can behold the one that is dear to me, that is all I want*. I hope you will excuse me for thus troubling you, but it really is my wish to get away from the company of the wicked: and, oh, may I serve Lord Jesus and bless his name for ever: that adorable God has brought me into existence, whatever my fate. I am, yours etc., Edwin

P.S. Please excuse the badness of the paper'.

* This refers to his twin brother, who had also been confined (elsewhere, on Orkney?), but had since died: no one had informed Edwin?

Miss Watson visited the island again in 1833 and Edwin attended prayer meetings, but was still subject to 'the same vexatious maltreatment'.

Though George had but recently returned to his wife and children, and the 'flesh' recoiled at the idea of a journey of 1500 miles, there and back, requiring much time and expense, and he had but £8 in the world, George remembered the text:

"Seek ye first the kingdom of God and his righteousness; and all things shall be added unto you: take therefore no thought of the morrow, for the morrow shall take thought for the things of itself: sufficient unto the day is the evil thereof."

He realised that he would be coming up against titles, wealth, self-interest, hired lawyers, bailiffs, timid – even treacherous – boatmen – all arrayed in a federal combination against him. But 'the fire burned within him' and he said "I will undertake the task". They had applied for Habeas Corpus in England, but this matter concerned Scotland. They were also concerned that Habeas Corpus might alert the opposition, too. George did not want to use Habeas Corpus, as he wanted to obtain Edwin's release through the hand of God, not Man. However, he agreed to carry a Habeas Corpus document to be used only as a last resort. They agreed that he should lecture only in Shetland and that they would pay his travelling expenses, to which he agreed.

Edwin had served in the Army, quartered in the East Indies. He had refused to fight a duel, whether from conscience or fear of being killed, it remains unknown. He had felt obliged to quit the service. His father, the Earl, was indignant of the disgrace on his return, banishing him from his presence. Edwin first resided with a gentleman in the west of England, but they quarrelled. His father then sent him with a letter, the contents of which were unknown to him, from Gloucestershire to Shetland, without any companion. He delivered the letter, a proof of his sanity. It seems that he was originally rather irascible, but had decided to submit mildly to his father's wishes. He had no money, presumably, and there was little else he could do. He was deprived of all his money and kept 'as a lunatic'. The father was now dead, being succeeded after 10 years, by his eldest son. It emerges that the father did leave him £150 per annum (a not inconsiderable sum in those days) in his will, with no condition that he should remain on Papa Stour. He was also left some freehold lands, probably personal property. Edwin was fourth son, and as such not entitled to inherit any of his father's estate, otherwise. From papers at the British Library, it appears that the Earl in question was the Earl of Balcarres, and Edwin was the Hon. Edwin Lindsay. It is understandable that the Earl was affronted by Edwin's refusal to fight, for he had himself served with distinction in America and fought a duel with Benedict Arnold, with no fatal injuries!

His brother, the present Earl, in a later exculpatory letter to the 'public' said:

> *'Suffice it then to say that after having been tried both in the navy and the military service and found incompetent to remain in either, or to conduct himself in the common usages of life, my father placed him, with his own consent, about 25 years ago, with a most worthy and respectable gentleman in Papa Stour, in the island of Shetland, where he had the full range and complete personal liberty, which he cannot have had elsewhere.'*

Gideon Henderson, his 'keeper' there, declared "That for a long series of years the petitioner has had charge and custody of keeping the Honourable Edwin, the youngest son of the deceased Earl, and the said Edwin not being of sound mind, the petitioner held the most strict injunctions from the deceased Earl, and now holds from the present Earl, to prevent the said Edwin from leaving the said Island of Papa Stour".

Edwin's brother, the executor of the deceased Earl's will, was directed to pay the sum to his order or receipt. There was no exception in the will on the grounds of insanity. Despite being the executor, the brother had apparently done nothing.

Edwin had apparently submitted when only 22 years of age, at a time when the demands of a father demanded instant submission and he was very dependent on his bounty, being ignorant of any professional calling or trade. To escape once in Papa Stour would be to 'beard starvation by a conflict with a merciless world.'

There is not the slightest evidence that he was insane or incompetent to conduct himself in the common usages of the world! Gideon Henderson must have known this, but this respectable gentleman was probably well paid for his keepership, and went along with this pretence.

George notes that Edwin had a mind 'so wanting in courage and intrepidity that even an enterprise less bold than an attempt to escape would have alarmed him'. He did at first resist the humiliation by his tormentors on Papa Stour, but found that resistance caused them to triumph, so he patently submitted to a madman's discipline. He went in and out, ate and drank, at the bidding of Gideon and his family, with the docility of a dog. We get a picture a man, not at all insane, but of a highly nervous disposition. He was kept entirely ignorant of his right to receive £150 per annum: perhaps surprisingly, he did not go insane under his torments, but adopted a religious turn of mind 'in the barren hills of Papa Stour'.

George, though in no way pardoning the two Earls, believed that a story circulating at the time of the subsequent law case that the stratagem was to preclude him from a large estate was erroneous. The primary cause was to have offended the pride of his father, the Earl: and the indifference of his brother kept him there, out of sight and out of mind. George did not consider that there was an element of deliberate fraudulence (though the failure of his brother, as executor, to deliver his inheritance was surely criminal?).

....

17. George Pilkington sets off for Shetland

George Pilkington sailed on the steam-ship Soho to Leith on 11.7.1835. A stranger invited him to attend Sunday worship on board, and he turned out to be a Member of Parliament 'involved with me in the duty that devolved on us during this interesting occasion.' This cryptic note suggests that Parliamentary interest had become involved in the freeing of Edwin. George stayed with a person to whom he had an introduction but kept secret his purpose. There was therefore some surprise that he would be lecturing in far-way Shetland, when 'there was so much to be done in the rest of Scotland'. He did lecture at Dalkeith and Leith. A lady, a guest of his host, told the company that Earl Balcarres had been alerted by Miss Watson's interest in Edwin's confinement and had caused Henderson, his 'keeper', to obtain certification of his state of mind from some 'respectable persons'.

George sailed in a schooner for Lerwick on 25.7.1835, and on arrival lodged at a hotel owned by the Captain's brother. Lerwick at that time had 3000 inhabitants and the streets were crooked and narrow, and not navigable by vehicles, of which there was apparently only one on the Island. The town was permeated by the smell of fish. The ordinary people were miserably poor, and obsequious to the precocious lairds, the needy possessors of those barren, treeless lands. The idol, 'Rank', was worshipped here as everywhere, even if clothed in the tattered, distinguishing garment of assumed haughtiness. George lectured here to the Friends, 450 persons attending, and at the Independent Chapel, where 700 attended. He also lectured at Scalloway. On his journey on foot about twenty miles to Scalloway and Sandness, from where there was a 1.5 mile boat trip across to Papa Stour, they crossed with difficulty many peat diggings, many being worked, and the women passed carrying great baskets of peat tethered to their backs. He thought this an oppressive custom, but noted that they seemed quite happy in this task. The ladies of the Friends were travelling on the backs of Shetland ponies, a much better way of travel across this terrain.

Reaching Scalloway, a large harbour sheltered by a number of islands, George noted that even in this retired spot, human beings ignorant of metropolitan magnificence, were nevertheless subject to all its vanities: the 'turfbog' lairds, rustic gentry, laboured to maintain their place or station, amid a rugged tenantry, just as 'the queen and nobles in this empire's court and capital!' The ruins of an ancient castle on an eminence above this insignificant town, reminded George of the folly of seeking treasures on Earth.

The laird invited him to dinner, showing him before dinner his dwarf trees, fenced by a 100 foot square of stone walling. He took some pride in this display, though they could not thrive in this barren soil (the winds of Shetland's west coast were surely also a factor in their stunted growth?). George gladly took leave of his:

'Neat little garden, with weeds o'errun,
And beautiful fish-pond, dried up by the sun'.

He lectured to about 150 people, and J.M., who lodged with him at the principle inn, proposed to accompany him to Papa Stour. George, at length, told him of the real purpose of his visit. J.M., who appears to have belonged to the Moravian church, was amazed that such a thing could be perpetrated in a Free Country and expressed an even greater desire to accompany him. In the middle of the night he laughed and said that George should give a lecture, meanwhile he would slip off with Edwin in a boat.

They next hired a boat and went to Rewick, from where they had to walk 3 miles to lecture in a Methodist chapel at the top of a mountain, a very small building with no built floor and very rough seating. 60 persons attended. The people here lived in what were little more than hovels.

At 9 pm they left on foot for the town of Walls, about 5 miles distant, over peat cuttings and bogs, and through a Scotch Mist: they passed two bays before at last reaching the bay of the town of Walls, where they knocked up the Methodist minister in the middle of the night. George admits that he was exhausted by this time. The minister's wife and two daughters provide a meal, and were surprised that George, now forgoing fish, flesh or fowl, supped on oatmeal cake and milk.

The Methodist minister at Walls said that George would be permitted to lecture on the Sabbath. He asked:

'Can you speak more than once in the day?'

'Oh, yes, 4 or 5 times if it be required of me.'

'Then you may lecture 3 times tomorrow in lieu of my sermons, and I will listen to you, as I desire to know all that I can about the subject.'

George lectured at 11 am in the Chapel at Walls, had a hasty dinner, and then walked 8 miles to Sandness, where his lecture closed at 6 pm. He then took a boat to Papa Stour, where he was to lecture again at 7 pm.

The minister had a friend at Papa Stour, who would accommodate him. George recognised the name of Edwin's 'keeper', Gideon Henderson, and said he would lodge elsewhere, but the minister said that Gideon would feel slighted if he did so. He met this gentleman in the Methodist chapel at Walls, wearing the dress of the superior order of gentry, a man of stature and muscle. His manner indicated that he regarded George as a person not even of minor importance. He said:

'I thank you Captain for your interesting lecture' and offered him accommodation in his house, though as this was the fishing season, he himself had to remain engaged at Walls. He would write to his sister, who kept his house for him, and his son.

On the journey to Sandness, of about 8 miles, a Shetland pony, diminutive like the local cattle, was provided for the accommodation of those who came to preach - the circuit, the minister added humorously, was 'priest-ridden'. George found the pony difficult to mount and soon tumbled off onto the ground. The pony knew he was a stranger and tried to get away. It was provided with a special bridle that prevented it grazing en route. It made several attempts to return home, and in the end George dismounted and walked the rest of the way. At last he had a view of Papa Stour, noting the forbidding coastline and the house showing up white in the distance; it had a clear view of the channel. His boots were saturated by the time they arrived at Sandness. After his lecture, he was rowed to Papa Stour, but they were delayed by leaving a parcel behind, and he apparently did not lecture that evening.

Besides his hostess the sister, the son, W.Henderson, (aged about 25) and two brothers and two sisters entered the room, returning from chapel. Then a tall, stout person with red hair and an unshaven beard entered, with a dejected countenance and in shabby attire. He was introduced as 'a stranger, sir, who is an inmate of our family'. George realised that this was Edwin.

20. Lerwick: the narrow streets are much the same as in George Pilkington's time.

21. Scalloway, with the castle visible and the steep, bare terrain which George Pilkington traversed on foot and with Shetland ponies.

18. On Papa Stour

In conversation Edwin asked if George was a minister of the gospel, to which George replied that he was a disciple, and that no man had made him a minister. He replied: 'Some imagine that no person can be a minister, except he be ordained by man: but in my opinion, no man can be a minister, except he be made so by the Lord'. When George stated his views on the illegality of war, Edwin disputed his views, showing himself shrewd in argumentation. When Edwin left the room for a moment, the hostess asked George if he did not observe that Edwin was mad. George replied in the negative.

'Oh, I can assure you that the poor man is quite insane: at times he is very violent: he is the brother of Earl Balcarres.'

When Edwin returned, George noted that he was allowed a portion of spirits to drink, though in Edinburgh, the lady S.W., had said that alcohol excited him to 'acts of phrenzy' George did not drink, as he was a member of the Temperance Society.

Next morning he met Edwin on a morning walk and asked him if he was happy; Edwin answered in the affirmative, but with an air of resignation. He then asked him if he felt any inclination to leave the island, Edwin answered:

'Yes, certainly, but I have no means of so doing.'

The conversation was interrupted. George had a later walk with the son, but Edwin was absent: he saw an ingenious system of water mills, which were powered by the same stream flow, in succession, and were used for grinding the corn. He estimated that the island was three and a quarter miles long and two wide and much exposed to the weather. He was told that in storms the spray is blown across the island from sea to sea. There were innumerable sea-gulls and wild geese, and seals were occasionally seen on the coast. He had a close encounter with an angry sea-gull.

'The very birds of the air rebuke me, thought he' (for his anxiety): He concluded that he must leave the outcome of his mission to his heavenly Father.

He met E.J., an elder, who maintained his family on an annual salary of £15, paid by Gideon Henderson for running the school. This man had signed the certification that Edwin was insane, but George realised that he was not in a position to go against his employer; the other signatory was a poor boatman. George realised that the document was of little worth. He also met Edwin going to the meeting, and gave him Miss Watson's letter to him. At the meeting he addressed 40 persons in the Methodist chapel;   Edwin belonged to the Methodist sect. Later he asked Edwin to meet him next morning – they had to talk in French, which Edwin understood, as they were being overheard. Edwin told him that Gideon Henderson would lose money by his departure, but that when he got his inheritance, he would recompense him. This was an extraordinary example of 'Love your enemy', particularly as it emerged that Gideon had at times beaten him.

George then wrote a protest document in three copies (one for Gideon Henderson, one for his son) and Edwin agreed to sign it. At breakfast, George told the company that he had something to communicate. He told them that he had come from London expressly to see Edwin, who had been held there for 25 years under a plea of lunacy: that he considered him quite sane. He showed them Gideon's letter, with the certification by the two people mentioned above: and said it was quite worthless. W. Henderson was surprised and shocked that George had obtained his father's letter. Edwin now presented the protest:

'To Gideon and W. Henderson

I hereby protest against your proceedings in illegally detaining me on this island, contrary to my will, and in direct violation of the law of the land: I call upon you to produce your authority, or stand to, and abide by all the consequences of falsely imprisoning me, without cause or power to do so, from any jury or other persons, who are or have been judges, or civil officers of the nation.

I present this to you in the presence of witnesses: and demand as a free British subject, your immediate reply, this 4th day of August 1835. Signed Edwin-----
Witnessed John. M., G. Pilkington'

George asked by whose order Edwin had been detained. W. Henderson said that it was by the order of the late Earl. George replied that the dead could not authorise the living. W. Henderson then claimed the authority of his brother, the present Earl, but George said that he had not seen Edwin for 25 years and thus could not tell whether or not he should still be confined. George asked if a jury had seen him, whether the Sheriff had visited him. The answer was negative, as it was whether Gideon Henderson was a licensed keeper. George then asked to be provided with a boat to take him away. The hostess protested that Edwin was in shabby clothes, and made his clothes dirty, and could not go like that (a delaying tactic?), but George answered that he had plenty of brothers and sisters in Christ who would see to his attire. Edwin said he was ready to go and they should order the boat. W. Henderson asked what he should tell his father and George replied that Edwin was 47 years old and thought he could take care of himself. The boat was ordered, a lot of the inhabitants who had somehow got wind of the affair were outside, and George addressed them and asked them not to circulate any reports that were injurious to Gideon Henderson and his family: and reminded them of his own principles of forgiving one's enemy. Many of Edwin's old acquaintances pressed on him to take farewell, and it was clear that he had many friends among the local populace. The schoolmaster, who had signed the certification letter, actually assisted George to board the boat. So he, J.M. and Edwin departed from Papa Stour.

22. Papa Stour, showing the comparatively good land there.

19. More hazards leading to the Sheriff Court at Lerwick

The boat passed the point of Sandness and landed at the Bay of Dale, where the minister/schoolmaster touched his hat and asked for the fare, 5 shillings and 6 pence, which was paid. They moved on to Walls across the peat-bogs. Having been warned of their arrival, Gideon Henderson came out and reluctantly read the document which Edwin presented to him. He asked George what his authority was for taking Edwin away: George replied that his only authority was a Christian heart. Gideon turned pale when asked whether his house was licensed to keep a madman. George knew that victory was his, he said:

'If you be his keeper, lay your hands on him'
'I am as respectable a man as you are. Sir: I am no keeper'

George told him that he knew Edwin would not resist him physically, if he laid his hands on him. He then said: 'Farewell' There was a lot of scuffling with a man sent by Gideon Henderson, before Edwin said:

'No person is taking me away. I am a free British subject and no man shall take me back or forth contrary to my will.'

To cut a long story short, George guaranteed the crew against seizure of their boat by any legal proceedings and they pushed off; in vain Gideon Henderson said that two peace officers were coming. They left at 4 pm on the 17 mile trip to Scalloway'. One of the rowers said: 'Mr Edwin, I do not think you remember me: I was a little boy when you first arrived here; you were then very fond of swimming, and carried me on your back in the water'. The breeze blew from the northwest, so they used the sail through the mist to

Scalloway. The charitable crew lent Edwin clothing to protect him from the cold, though George thought that he was very hardy. They reached Scalloway at 7 pm and had a very refreshing tea at the Inn where George had lodged previously, and afterwards gave thanks to the 'Shepherd' who had brought them so far.

They arranged to sail for Orkney at 2 am. J.M., despite George's protestations, agreed to go to Lerwick and fetch George's baggage, which had been left there; he said that he wanted to do something useful towards such a worthy cause.

After they had retired to their room, Gideon and his son were heard climbing the stairs, and George Pilkington barred the door to them, saying that it was his private apartment. Gideon apologised for some violent language earlier on, and said that he was unconcerned in the matter, and just desired a document to satisfy the Earl; George said that he was not the least offended by him. George suspected that some other reason had brought Gideon 17 miles away from his 'very important business' at Walls, at such an hour and in such weather.

After this he and Edwin read psalm 91 together, and prayed. Edwin slept in the bed, while George kept watch. At half past one the landlady knocked up George with his baggage, which had arrived; she said that she had heard Edwin praying in the night, and thought that it was a shame to treat him as a madman.

The sloop was ready and they embarked to it on a small boat, rowed by an aged man and his strong, muscular daughter of 19 years of age. They passed fleets of fishing boats and then the wind dropped to almost 'breathlessness', and a rowing boat came straight for them. The captain said 'I do not like that boat'. Edwin kept out of the way in the cabin, and the boat came alongside. A constable advanced, asking:

'Where is the captain of this sloop?'

'Here, sir,' replied the captain.

'I seize this vessel for sailing to the Orkney's without permission.'

Then he turned to George: 'You are my prisoner,' he said, and the same to Edwin, who then emerged.

George asked why he had seized the sloop:

'Because you sailed to Orkney without a license.'

George answered that he could not arrest him for intending to do something, just as one could not arrest a man for intending to do murder. He also pointed out that they were at sea, not on Shetland, but the constable replied that the Sheriff was also the Admiral. George replied that, if so, by custom the arrest had to be made with a silver oar, but the Constable said that 'they did not do things that way in Zetland'. He said:

'My duty is to seize the vessel and let the court decide on the merits of the case.'

When George asked what authority he had, he replied; 'Here is my warrant, you may read it, but I cannot let you have possession of it.'

It read:

> *'Petition of Mr Gideon Henderson, with concourse of the Procurator Fiscal, against George Pilkington and the Hon. Edwin Lindsay.*
>
> *Lerwick 4th August 1835*
>
> *Unto the Honourable Sheriff of the County of Orkney and Zetland, and his substitute of Zetland. The petition of Gideon Henderson, residing in the Island of Papa Stour,*

with the concourse of the Procurator Fiscal in the public interest.

Humbly sheweth:-

That for a long period of years, by-past, the petitioner has had charge, custody and keeping of the Honourable Edwin, a younger son of the deceased Earl of Balcarrres; and the said Edwin not being of sound mind, the petitioner held the most strict injunctions from the deceased Earl, and now holds from the present Earl, to prevent Edwin from leaving the said island of Papa Stour, or going anywhere without the petitioner's consent.

That, not withstanding thereof, a person calling himself George Pilkington, who lately arrived in Zetland, and visited Papa Stour, has most unwarrantably and illegally, forcibly carried off the person of the said Edwin from the petitioner's house in Papa Stour, and from that island itself, and without communicating his attention to the private petitioner, much less producing any authority for such a proceeding.

That, understanding, the said George Pilkington is about instantly carrying from Zetland, the said Edwin from Scalloway, where he now is, the present application is imperatively necessary.

May it therefore please your lordships to grant warrant to your officers of court, to bring back to the private petitioner and place in his custody, the person of the said Edwin; and to apprehend and bring before your lordships for examination, the person of the said George Pilkington; and in the event of him not being able to produce any authority for taking away the said Edwin, to interdict, prohibit and discharge him from doing so, and to obtain your officers to assist the private petitioner in carrying the said Edwin back to Papa Stour, therein to remain until further orders; or otherwise do according to justice, & c.

Signed Gideon Henderson
Signed James Greig, P.F., grants his concourse
"Taw 5ᵗʰ August 1835"

The sheriff substitute having considered this petition, grants warrants to the sheriff's officers to apprehend the said Edwin, wherever he can be found within this jurisdiction and re-place him in the custody of the petitioner, until farther orders: and further grants warrants to the sheriff's officers to apprehend the said George Pilkington, and bring him before me for farther examination.

Signed Andrew Duncan
"Lerwick 5ᵗʰ August 1835"

……….……………….……..

20. Justice is done at Lerwick Sheriff Court

They arrived at Scalloway and were once again inmates of the Beer Shop Inn, where the landlady seemed much alarmed to see them return in such inauspicious circumstances. The constable asked whether they would like to ride to Lerwick, the quickest but longest route, so George ordered three ponies and was just about to pay 4s 6d for their hire, when a stranger pointed out that he should not pay when a prisoner. This left the constable in a quandary, for he was ready to pay for their ponies, but thought that he would not be able to claim the 1s 6d for his pony, so he said he would walk beside them. George then pointed out to him that he and Edwin would escape by cantering off if he did this, so he ordered a third pony. At Tingwall a kind clergyman invited them in for refreshment.

On approaching Lerwick they observed members of the 'upper classes' watching them with spy-glasses, and George felt humbled by being so escorted as a prisoner through such an uncourteous mob.

He then asked the constable if he was to go to the gaol, and the latter seemed quite shocked by this suggestion, so George asked to go to his former lodging (apparently prisoners in the gaol kept a key with them, which George thought 'spoke volumes for the poor of these islands'). Edwin made poor use of the razor, and a barber was called to trim his beard, he being now dressed in a clean neckcloth, his coat brushed and his shoes well polished.

They were conducted to the courthouse, where a 'person of importance' was seated at a table, with Gideon and W. Henderson in attendance. The unknown grandee, with an air of reproof, this addressed George:

'Sir! You acted very improperly by interfering in such a cruel manner with the peace of a private family.'

'I did nothing more than an act of justice which British law will recognize; for Edwin was illegally and unjustly deprived of his liberty.'

'Sir, you shall soon see that British laws will not answer in this country, and that you shall not come up here to act as you please.'

'If your laws sanction such proceedings, the sooner they are changed for British laws, the better. But I desire to know by what law you have arrested me.'

'I did not arrest you: I am your prosecutor, Sir: I am the Procurator Fiscal.'

'Oh, I'm not surprised at your strange opinions about my conduct: I thought that you were the Sheriff; and that I was in his court.'

Then rising to go away, he said: 'Stop, Sir. Constable, he is your prisoner.'

'I am indeed a prisoner: but you'll soon be glad to let me go.'

'Constable, take the man away.'

This legal buffoon, who must have been James Greig, and who was obviously a crony of Gideon Henderson, was very soon to have a shock. At the Court, the Sheriff treated George civilly, summoning the other parties except Edwin. George explained his mission and his manner of recovery of Edwin, and protested at the false imprisonment. He said that he was not employed by anyone; he had acted of his own freewill, merely to assist a fellow Christian. He said that he was not willing to go without seeing Edwin have the rights of a British subject. He admitted that he had intended to go to Orkney, and had been further impressed with Edwin's sanity, hearing him declare that he would give the family of Gideon Henderson an annual stipend.

The Sheriff said: 'You may go where you please, Sir. I have no further occasion with you.'

A ridiculous situation now arose with George saying that he had been wrongly imprisoned and he would not go! The Sheriff said 'But Sir, I have no further power to keep you!'

To this George said: 'You should have thought of this before you arrested me. I now have an action for damage against all parties involved.'

The reply was 'I know that, Sir, but not in this court.'

It emerged that Edwin, also, was not now a prisoner and could spend the day with him. The Sheriff's men civilly had given Edwin intoxicating drinks, and George reproved him for drinking, but he said he could respectfully submit his case to the Sherriff, which he did. He declared to the court that he had frequently expressed the desire to leave Papa Stour, and it was now his wish to go. He wished to go with Mr Pilkington, and positively refused to return to Papa Stour. The Sheriff Substitute declared that his detention since arrival in Shetland had no legal or judicial authority: the court had no power to prevent him leaving Shetland.

George had promised to give a second lecture at Lerwick, which he did at 6pm, and at 8pm on 6th August 1835 was told that the brig of 250 tons, the King's Packet, was ready to leave for Peterhead. Apparently Edwin, at the last moment, then informed him that he was not coming with him. His reasons are best summed up in a Newspaper article, which George read later, while in Liverpool and a quote from J.B.

'Although I declined accompanying the gentleman who undertook my rescue, yet having recovered some scruples that possessed my mind at the time, I prayed to God for strength, and availed myself of the next opportunity, and being restored to liberty am prepared to claim my just legal rights.' (London, November 1835).

This agrees with what he told George at the time, previous to his departure:

'I have offended God: I am not worthy of you.'

In reminiscences of his life, left in the hand of J.B., a friend of George, he wrote:

'I saw that I was a great sinner in the sight of God, and therefore I declined going into the packet, rather wishing to punish myself than go; but, however I got up my spirits and prayed to God to give me strength for I needed it; indeed I needed to be with God in this great undertaking, the deliverance from tyranny, and my establishment for life.'

Edwin's scruples may have been about the fact that he did not entirely agree with George's viewpoint on military service and war: his father had been a very distinguished soldier, and he still respected him to a degree, and he himself had served in the Army for four years.

In the event the actions of George Pilkington, achieved the overthrowing of the justification for his detention, showing it to be illegal: he was shortly after brought away from Shetland, but only after some scurrilous actions by his 'keeper' and his cronies, which totally gainsaid Gideon Henderson's pious protestations of disinterest to George. How this happened does not directly concern George Pilkington, but is briefly recounted in the next chapter.

George received much acclamation from those attending his lecture on that day and after it was acclaimed from the shore, until the vessel was out of hearing. He wrote 'Farewell beloved oppressed poor of Shetland.'

....

21. The conclusion of the Edwin interlude

George had travelled 64 miles, mostly on foot in Shetland, and delivered 7 lectures, besides freeing Edwin. The vessel experienced the 'heaviest tempest' that he had ever met in his sea voyages, scudding under bare poles all the way to Peterhead, from whence he took a coach to Aberdeen, where he gave two lectures and on to

Edinburgh. He arrived at London having travelled 1508 miles, addressed 6620 persons on peace and 800 parents and teachers on their responsibilities. He was very unsatisfied at not being accompanied by Edwin, and wrote saying that he must not be too pleased with his efforts; the success achieved was due to the Almighty, and he acknowledged the great help by J.M., who was the young son of a Moravian minister.

He did not know it, but Edwin had been plied with drinks while he was lecturing in Lerwick, by one James Mout, the brother in law of Gideon's sister. Somehow, they had contrived to make him write the message saying that he did not wish to accompany George. Within two days they had brought him back to Papa Stour, where, having no money, he was unable to leave as before.

George meanwhile lectured at Stoke Newington and Tottenham. A friend, E.B., had collected £20 in gifts to him from various sources and some other smaller gifts meant that he had £36 in his pocket, which allowed him to pay off all minor debts and stay at home for a period to write up his first book. He must have been exhausted after his experiences in Shetland at the age of 50 years.

The outcome of Edwin's return to confinement is well told in a short book entitled 'The Earl of Balcarres and the Hon. Mr Lindsay' by 'Ebenezer' (a pseudonym, probably by J.M.). Catharine Watson wrote several letters to Edwin, with no reply: she therefore returned to Shetland, where she obtained the service of the Sheriff's Officer (the 'constable' previously mentioned, who was the 'active and intelligent Leonard Henry'). With an order demanding Gideon Henderson to give up Catharine Watson's letters to them, together they went to Papa Stour, where Gideon denied receiving any letters (he was apparently among other things a confirmed liar). Leonard Henry told him that he was taking Edwin to the mainland of Shetland, Gideon, amazingly, despite the Sheriff's previously ruling, said that he would not allow that (he retained his implicit belief in the Earl's superior authority to the last!). Leonard Henry than said that he would obtain a Sheriff's order, and Gideon then had to give way. The Sheriff's court ruled as before, and Edwin asked for Leonard Henry to accompany him to London, which he did via Scalloway, Orkney and the steamboat Velocity to Leith. Only when he had seen Edwin safely lodged with a friend in London, did Leonard Henry return to Shetland.

Within two days, Catharine Watson had briefed a reliable solicitor to present Edwin's case for payment of all the money owed to him in his father's will.

George Pilkington disagreed with going to law, as he believed the gospel forbade a disciple to do so, but Catharine Watson, 'could not see the safety in this'. Anyway, Edwin would have had no funds if he had not done so.

The following facts emerge from the 'Ebenezer' account:

1) Catharine Watson initially found Edwin dressed in clothes of indescribable wretchedness: he had been spat on by the children of Gideon Henderson in the past.

2) The Earl of Balcarres published a rambling letter in the Albion on 11.11.1835 which was full of mis-statements: the most important being the statement that Edwin had returned to Papa Stour willingly, and that he was perfectly happy and contented there.

3) Balcarres stated that Edwin was a twin and the family thought it expedient to consult the celebrated Dr Willis (one of George the Thirds absurd medical advisers!) and Dr Baillie, who said that there was a malformation of the head which destroys intellect and it would get worse: phrenology was then in fashion in medical circles: it is unclear

whether these medical boobies thought all twins were so afflicted, but as Edwin served 4 years in the army in India, for the noble Earl to cite this was absurd.

4) His twin brother had been placed with another 'respectable gentleman' in Orkney and died in two years before: we simply do not know if he was insane when confined or became so because of his confinement, or was never insane.

5) The noble Earl said that Edwin had been found incompetent in both navy and army, but he had served four years in the latter, and only left because he refused to fight a duel.

6) The noble Earl had not visited him once since his father died a decade before and could not possibly have known of his condition. His father had been kinder to Edwin and said that he could accompany Gideon Henderson on his business elsewhere in Shetland. The present Earl claimed that he had been overseas much of the time. This was no excuse for withholding the money due to Edwin from his father's will.

7) The Earl blackened the name of the Methodists and Quakers, and George Pilkington: in fact the Quakers or 'Friends' had the motto 'Do good by stealth, and blush to find it fame': all these people had wanted was to see Edwin receive justice.

This he did in the Court of Chancery on August 6th 1836, in the case Lindsay versus the Earl of Balcarres. The Earl repeated his rambling and lame story, bringing in again the 'wise doctors' and the 'head-bumps'! It seems possible that either the Earl himself was not very bright, or he thought himself above the law. The vice chancellor said that there was an inconsistency in the conduct of the Earl of Balcarres that it was quite impossible for him to reconcile. He could not very well understand how he raised the present objection to suing out a commission for the protection of his alleged insane brother, on the ground of inability to discover his present place of abode, when he must for a period of twenty years have known the place and circumstances under which he was living.

It emerged that the Earl of Balcarres, Edwin's father, died possessed of personal property worth upwards of £130,000 and real estate yielding £5000-£6000 per annum. The sum due to Edwin was only £580. 'The greatest excitement and indignation prevailed in the court during the progress of this argument'. Edwin was granted this patrimony to which he was entitled, due to the actions of a counsel of unflinching integrity and courage. 'Ebenezer' mentions the reproach and shame on the Earl inherent in this judgment and quotes Tacitus:

'Acerrima proximorum odia.'

(The hatred of those who are near to us is most violent')

'Ebenezer' adds a note on Edwin's twin brother Richard, who was probably cruelly treated in Orkney and died, with no inquest or judicial inquiry, no one shedding a tear at his grave.

Of Gideon Henderson, he described him as 'utterly contemptible, and this also must apply to his family: he also would be subjected to heavy penalties according to the law of Shetland for becoming Edwin's gaoler and keeper. Edwin made a noble speech to the court, refusing to take further action, because it was up to the Almighty to punish, not him.

'Ebenezer' said 'Of Captain Pilkington it is impossible to say too much, or of the untiring patience of Miss Watson. As far as worldly remembrances go, Captain George Pilkington and Miss Watson will live in the memories of all who keep the commandments of Christ and walk in his ways.'

The last words on this interlude come from George Pilkington, who heard from his friend J.B.: that it was particularly gratifying to his friends that they observed a progressive and striking improvement in Edwin's manner and general behaviour, since his re-introduction to society. He had exhibited a benevolent disposition and was by no means an uninteresting companion. His remarks were pointed and pertinent: and above all he was under the influence of religious impressions. It was suggested that but for his illegal confinement, he might have filled no mean part among his friends. George adds the hope that that he would take to drinking only water: it is clear that he had a weakness with strong drink (and the Scots drink largely spirits): it is not known whether he took this advice! Here, we lose sight of Edwin: we can only hope that his declining years were peaceful in the company of his Methodist and Quaker friends. The Earl probably had not the slightest twinges of conscience: in 1848 he took the title, 1st Earl of Crawford and he lived on to be an octogenarian dying in 1869. We do not know whether, his 'creature' ('Ebenezer's words, not mine), Gideon Henderson, was ever charged under Shetland Law for his criminal confinement of Edwin.
....

22. Back to lecturing marathons

It is important to realise that George Pilkington's lecturing itineraries occupied two years prior to the Edwin interlude, and his next set, within England, occupied a further two and a half years, whereas the Edwin interlude, which he described in great detail, occupied only three months.

After a month at home, George embarked on a new route starting at Luton on 15th November 1835. In Luton, he informed his listeners that he had found no rest for his conscience until he had sent his military uniform out of the house. This is an example of a tendency to rationalise his experiences into the framework of his pacifism, for he had of course got rid of his uniform (reluctantly?), much earlier on, when lacking the funds for a decent meal. It is also worth mentioning that throughout his life he used the title 'Captain', to which he was entitled (and strangely I am, though never have used it since WW2): though this is understandable, as it was an age when it was important to have the distinction of a 'Gentleman's rank'.

He had some opposition on this itinerary: at an unnamed town a pastor quoted at him 'pugilistically': "The rule is 'as far as you live peacefully with all men'; and when we cannot do so, we read that 'these are the keepers of the house'. The Pastor obviously believed that it was not practical to adhere always to the first rule. In another town, another clergyman declaimed: 'Had not God called me to the exercise of war in which spiritual weapons are employed, I can see no reason why I should not wear a red or blue coat, and fight the battles of my country... In my judgement the Peace Society is visionary and vain'. He conceived that Cornelius, the Centurion and first Gentile Convert to Christianity, was a brave soldier. Another objection received was: 'there is no war now: what is the point of such lectures'. George countered all these arguments, skilfully, but was clearly ruffled by them.

He did note, in a footnote, that Archdeacon Jeffreys, in a publication entitled: 'Charges against Custom and Public Opinion' had supported his viewpoint, but added 'But many a better man than I thinks otherwise'.

On the 2nd November 1835, he went to Runcorn by train (presumably the Liverpool and Manchester Railway), the first use of this mode of transport recorded by him: in fact, the railways were to be an important element in his last professional years. He got very cold waiting for a ferryboat to Runcorn. At both Preston and

Garstang, the Temperance Hotels refused to charge him for lodging. At the latter place a man selling a patent gingerbread by the roadside, and who had heard him lecture, presented him with a parcel of it. Though George protested, he eventually accepted it, and as he had no lunch with him, had a very welcome gingerbread lunch!

Fellow passengers on a coach pointed out to him that many things ordered in the scripture were not practicable these days: for example, 'travelling without purse or scrip'. George replied that he did exactly that. One wonders where he carried the small gifts of money that he received; and of course, the common traveller could not rely on the sort of small gifts and hospitality that a lecturer like himself could, and did, rely on. At Appleby, he found the audience very poor and distressed, and sorry that a man who could have given him some money was not present, yet they paid for his seat on the coach to Barnard Castle.

At Birmingham, he was offered a situation which would have ensured the livelihood of his family (possibly railway surveying?), but he could not at that time find it in his heart to give up his self-imposed itineraries for which he believed that God had called him, though there is some reason to believe that he did latter accept this offer.

He remained at home for two months, getting his book ready for the publishers, but gave four lectures locally: at Chatham, a number of military officers were present, but listened to him politely and attentively, until someone (foolishly?) cried 'Fire!' and the audience of 700 rushed out. He recalled a similar experience at Dewsbury, where he had just told his audience that several hundred tons of human and horse bones had been imported from the fields of Liepsic and Waterloo for the purpose of making manure (is this really true?), when one of the audience groaned in a fit, there were shrieks from the rest of the audience and a stampede, in which one gentlewoman vaulted over her pew to escape. Certainly it was not all easy going on these itineraries!

He commenced another itinerary on 1st March 1836, starting at Hitchin. At Melton Mowbray, the minister announced a collection from his pew, to George's embarrassment. At Hawkeshead, a naval officer admitted that he was converted to George's view that all war was illegal according to the Gospels. From Wark he had to walk 6 miles back to Hexham, where he had left his baggage, and covered the distance in an hour and twenty minutes, considering this not bad for a man of 51, subsisting on a diet of vegetables, milk and water (this seems almost incredible, and maybe the distance was exaggerated). At Allendale, he shared a pony with his host, the pony carrying two (this suggests that he was not himself of large build, as does his experiences with Shetland ponies). He stayed commonly at quite humble farmhouses or clerical dwellings, but at Haltwhistle he lodged in a mansion, attended on by a butler and footmen, at which he observed 'How diversified is the lot of man'.

This contrast clearly troubled him, but he came to the conclusion that the well-off could equally follow the path of righteousness as the poor.

At Carlisle, he declined to accept a gift from his host on parting, because the latter admitted not to be wholly convinced by his arguments about peace (he was always a stickler on this point), but he was at a loss when his host's wife offered him money saying that she was entirely convinced. He reluctantly accepted it so as not to hurt her feelings. At Earby, he lectured for two hours, whereupon his voice failed, becoming hoarse due to the cold. As he was later to talk to the children, he applied a mustard poultice to his throat, but before he could commence was sidetracked to lecture at Barnoldswick, only afterwards addressing 500 children and 500 parents at Earby, where he 'talked for an hour and a half with no problem in his voice'. It is interesting that in those days children were so controlled that they would listen attentively to a speaker for such a duration – one cannot envisage a modern children's audience sitting still for so long! And after this, they sang to him an as yet unpublished hymn 'Farewell', which he reproduced on the last page of his 1839 book. Returning to London on the 20th of June 1836, his throat was still inflamed, and he spent three months there working on his book for the publishers.

On return he lacked nothing to provide his family with food and lodging; and he had been clothed from head to foot by occasional gifts along his route.

Commencing his next route on about the 18th of August 1836, he had but £2 10s in his pocket when he embarked, so he took a steamboat to Hull and commenced at Darlington. His route took him through the Yorkshire Dales, along Wensleydale, through Bedale, Leyburn and Masham; the people were very poor here, but even so furnished him with his transport; even once in a butcher's cart and another time in a carrier's heavy wagon. After this, he returned home for a month.

He commenced a new route on 17th October 1836, commencing at Wetherby, and decided to go by steam-boat to Hull, to save money, but had a foreboding in a dream of a dangerous passage. Despite a restless mind, he stuck to the plan, rather than going overland by coach. He left London on 7th October and his wife and children accompanied him to the landing stage. His wife urged him to book in the cabin not the forecastle. When they reached the channel, at 8 pm, the wind blew very hard from the south, and at midnight there was a tremendous crash of the waves on deck, and the cabin passengers rushed about. 'Oh! What a dreadful night' said a passenger who had been talking earlier to George about his religious unbelief. Seeing that George was relatively undisturbed, trying to sleep amidst the hubbub, he said 'Oh! What it is to be a Christian! I see now its value'. He said that George's calmness and fortitude had turned one poor soul to Christ. So George, despite his forebodings, obtained a convert and they reached Hull safely, and took a steamboat on to Selby together, and George once again used the train, this time to Leeds.

At Tadcaster, he convinced a Captain of the Army of the unlawfulness of war. This man had been at the battle of Vimiera, fought on the Sabbath day, and the troops had been assembled for prayers, when the enemy came in sight. He said "We slurred over the prayers as quickly as possible, formed an alignment and fought the battle!"

At Leeds, he was denied the use of a chapel because a large concourse of people had twice before damaged the pews, so he had to pay £3 11s from his own pocket to hire the Assembly Rooms. This was a rare occurrence, he was almost always allowed the use of a chapel or hall free. After the lecture he received £19 10s 6d in gifts --- he always kept a record even down to the pennies ---and so was amply repaid for his outlay. Walking to Otley, he became very hungry, but saw a woman picking blackberries, so moving well away from her so as not to interfere with her picking, he picked some and had a blackberry lunch. Fortified, he lectured at Otley for 2 hours. He returned to London by the London Mail and the book-keeper said that the fare was 35s, but as he had enjoyed his lecture he would charge him 30s. He arrived at London lacking nothing. There he found an invitation from the Peace Society to become their Agent and Lecturer, but declined, because he thought that he had a higher duty: to exhort his audiences to: 'Be not faithless, but believe!'

He remained at home for 10 days and then commenced a new itinerary at Watford on the 20th December 1836. He was apparently so driven to his cause that he was prepared to leave home over Christmas, even for this short itinerary through Hertfordshire. However, there is no doubt at all that his wife supported him in his self-motivated crusade. He then rested at home for seven weeks.

He commenced another route on the 20th January 1837 starting at Hertford. At Cambridge he had a very bad reception, one or two of the audience getting up and leaving, and then most of them followed. He was much put out by this, having never experienced such deliberate discourtesy, but continued to the end. He remained at home for 17 days and then started a route at Maldon on 18th April 1837. Saxmundham, he described as having the reputation of being 'One of the darkest spots of the Empire, where no Christian effort had produced any effect'. But they came en masse to 'hear the truth', and he spoke for two hours, noting that 'Many of the high professors of Cambridge had fled in less than half this time!' I do not know why Saxmundham was so singled out; I lived close to it in my childhood and no trace of this stigma ever reached me! Returning home on 29th July, he stayed at home for 34 days and then started on a new route at Witham (see Table 3, inserted as an example). Then on 8th August he commenced the last in England of which we have any record at Stratford, returning home on 17th August 1838. He had now apparently decided to visit Ireland to lecture and visit his father's grave (he had never returned since joining the Royal Engineers at the turn of the century).

Table 3: Itinerary 15, an example of one of his itineraries

Town	Summary of details
Witham	20.6.1837 – 29.7.1837
Colchester	458 miles: 24 towns
Manningtree	31 lectures in 38 days on peace: to 8180 persons: to 350 on temperance
Harwich	Children addressed: 750
Ipswich	Parents and teachers: 100
Woodbridge	
Framlingham	
Wickham Market	
Yoxford	
Peasenhall	
Wrentham	
Harleston	
Gorleston	
Lowestoft	
Southwold	
Yarmouth	
Bungay	
Beccles	
Pulham	
Diss	
Eye	
Debenham	
Billericay	
Brentwood	

23. George Pilkington's own conclusions about his itineraries

George Pilkington was clearly slowing up during these last itineraries in England. He does not earlier mention his health, but probably his meagre diet was taking its toll. He also had to have an operation after returning home in August 1838; the nature of it is not stated, but it was related to an injury that he had received long ago in Sierra Leone. He decided to visit Ireland, both to visit his father's grave in Dublin and pursue an itinerary there.

Meanwhile, it is convenient to look at his own conclusions about his lecturing on peace and temperance, which were published in his first (1836) book, but covered much of his later itineraries in England. One thing noted in this is that he gives different figures for mileages, in his earliest itineraries. His persistent logging of his miles travelled and the numbers attending his lectures is remarkable and must relate to his engineer's training. However, he did make some such mistakes with his figures: for example, the distance from Wark to Hexham given above is wildly out. He did a lot of retracing his steps, which must have been tiresome, having to go to a town and arrange a meeting, putting out leaflets advertising it, and return days later to hold the meeting.

He says that he 'inquired into his motives' frequently, and 'the prejudice of the eye of scrutiny pierced him to the heart': 'indifference or contempt were as a cloud to darken his way'. He was up against a torrent of prejudice in favour of the long received doctrine that Christian men may bear weapons and serve in the wars. This was actually inscribed in the 39 Articles of the Church Faith, as the 37th Article, he noted.

He had the expenses of printing bills, of travelling, of his own necessities and supporting a family; the means for this were scanty but sufficient. He expended 'every farthing for the glory of God, and used nothing for himself beyond his needs'. He also remembered 'his poor brother' and gave as required to such charity.

He quoted:

'Man wants but little here below, nor wants that little long.'

He always found that whenever his resources dwindled, his store was replenished. He believed that his heavenly Father never suffered him to be empty. As his book title suggests, the root of his belief was Providence – that the deity was watching over him personally and his needs. He also believed that the same deity never let his store remain full. In saying this, he alludes to the fact that at the onset of his lecturing for organisations, he did intend to emigrate to Canada, but never was in any way able to build up sufficient funds, whether working for the Peace or other organisations, or on his own. We know now that he did emigrate eventually, but not for at least another ten years after 1838, and to South Africa, not Canada as originally intended.

After 4 years, he gave up intoxicating drinks, to save time and money, and in the belief that the mind is deprived by their use to seek spiritual gifts (this abstinence on occasion offended his hosts). After meeting a vegetarian at Liverpool on one of his itineraries, he was persuaded to become vegetarian: his wife also became vegetarian, but was later persuaded to abandon this regime on medical grounds. With this regime of abstinence, he travelled 8000 miles in 25 months, speaking at least 5 times per week and on one of his last trips gave 69 lectures in 73 days! His throat became affected latterly and he had pulsations in the chest, and this may be the reason he apparently gave up his lecturing in Britain after his visit to Ireland. He did not advise others on vegetarian diet, but left it to their choice.

Always the subject of his financial support was a sore point. He never had an organised collection, but early on did express willingness to receive anything that was offered. However, in September 1834 on leaving Leicester, a most conscientious person said that he believed that it was not consistent with his faith to do so. Always ready to adopt ideas from others, he then restricted himself to saying that he had undertaken his mission in faith, though his means were inadequate to his expenses. After January 1835, he mentioned nothing about his expenses and means, but unfortunately later that year was quoted in a laudatory fashion, attributing his strength wrongly to his riches. He therefore returned to mentioning his financial circumstances when appropriate in his lectures.

He closed with some statistics, which would involve duplication if reproduced here. He finally encouraged others to follow in his path:

'That they may help to arouse a slumbering people to the wickedness of Satan, who as a roaring lion walketh about, seeking whom he may devour.'

He obviously believed in Satan as a personified inspirer of wickedness.

24. Visit to Ireland

Because he had now to remain at home for several weeks, George's pecuniary resources became low;   however, some 'disciples' were 'inclined to remit money to him, by his heavenly father', so the family did not suffer.   He was now directed in a dream to visit Ireland.   He was always prone to take his dreams seriously, perhaps surprising in one who was in other ways a very practical man.   He had £5 left, so resolved to go by steamboat.   He contacted a friend, E.B., and asked him to convene a meeting of children and parents in Dublin on 5th November 1837.

Before leaving he attended a 'Friends' meeting – he seems by now to have had a very close affiliation with the Quakers, though not a member of the sect – and at this meeting a minister made a remark that implied that George was unwelcome there, whereupon he left the meeting in a huff.   His wife afterwards told him "Ah! George, You should not have left the meeting!   You went there to worship God – 'Great peace have they that love the law, and nothing shall offend them!'";   this affair caused him great regret and self-questioning, so he went to the same meeting on the next Sunday and apologised.   His wife told him at this time: 'George, you must now be guarded lest vain pride should again get the advantage of you and incline you to feel as if you had done great things today'.   This is very interesting: Charlotte had a mind of her own, and was not one to always go along with George's whims, though she fully supported his pilgrimage.

On the first of November he left Liverpool on a packet for Kingstown, from whence he took the train to Dublin (it is remarkable how the railways were already spreading far and wide as early as 1837). His letter had not reached E.B., so nothing had been arranged.

In the meanwhile, he visited his old home in Camden Street, just west of St Stephens Green: he had not seen it for 33 years. He knocked on the door and was allowed in, seeing his old rooms. It was a very sentimental return; he had been seen off at the quay by his father all those years ago, and had gone off in the spirit of youthful adventure, and never seen his father again. He looked out a widowed lady in a pastry-cook's shop, the only person who now remembered him and his father, who had died 30 years before. She said: 'Your father was a very benevolent man – everybody loved him, he was always doing good. But, sure, your stepmother was a proud woman! But, oh, how like your father you are. I remember you when you were this height. What a beautiful boy you were. Oh, but time has made a great change in you. I would hardly have known you again. I always observe that the handsomest of children grow up the ugliest of men!'

This remark, which slipped out, reminded George that his years of pilgrimage were fast approaching to an end. His next visit was to St. Peters Church, where his father, mother and siblings who had died before him were buried. We do not know if they were full brothers and sister or half brothers and sister. His father had died at the age of only 45.

E.B. invited George to stay with him, which meant that balance of 25s left to him was not encroached on. His kind host also offered to take his eldest son, George W. Pilkington, as an apprentice without fee. He accepted this offer and at once communicated it to his wife in London. He realised that it was a wrench for her to part with her eldest son, 'a youth who loved her even as he was loved'. Unfortunately we do not know E.B.'s nature of business, so in what George W. was apprenticed. It is likely it was building, for we know he later became a leading builder in South Africa.

119

Also George himself received at this time an anonymous note containing 30s, and three gifts of £1, so he was able to pay for the carriage of his parcels containing bills and his own expenses travelling after them.

His pilgrimage through Ireland was by no means untroubled, and he encountered bigotry from both Protestants and Catholics. He commenced at Wicklow (see Table 4). He first had problems at Ferns, where an individual who had principle control of the school room, the only venue in the town, refused its use at the last moment. George went to see him with his host there, and the individual said at once 'You may do so', and apologised for his refusal. George had a pleasant discussion with him, and the meeting was well attended. At Waterford, a 'disciple' travelling with him paid his hotel expenses. He started on the coach for Youghal at 7am, and to his surprise it did not stop for refreshments and he spent twenty four hours with only a biscuit and tea, before having his dinner at 4 pm. It is clear that he drank water only sparingly during his travels and this was probably having a severe effect on his general health.

At Tullow his lecture was disturbed by two known interrupters, with jokes and remarks of 'hear, hear'! He threatened several times to cease speaking, and told them of his conversion by a Roman Catholic Bishop in Trinidad, but they asked loudly: 'But what are you now?' He said that they must judge that from his words and that his only intention was to induce his countrymen to love one another. He did withdraw, but the Vicar, present with his family, asked him to return and lecture again at a meeting to which tickets would be issued to prevent interruption.

At Goree, however, the vicar and his family withdrew during his lecture, presumably objecting, as Protestants, to his account of his conversion by a Catholic Bishop. However, the landlord of the hotel waived his lodging expenses, wishing him to return, and there would be a meeting 'such as Goree had never before seen.'

He returned to Dublin on 7th December 1837 and met up with his son George William, who shared a room with him for 14 days, and at once turned earnestly to business. George delivered a peace lecture at Dr Urwick's meeting and another at Kingstown, besides attending three temperance lectures.

Setting off again, at Clara, the meeting place was too small and he addressed his audience for one and a half hours in the moonlight and frosty night from the top of a flight of steps; they were mostly Roman Catholics, but heard him to the end.

Not so at Tullamore, where, in the Court House, he only commenced speaking when there was a hideous yell, accompanied by a cry 'Let all good Catholics leave the place!'. About 150 ran out from all directions, but three times as many stayed to the end, though 'one misguided person attempted to drown down my voice'.

At Edenderry about 500 persons, again mainly Roman Catholics, listened to the end and the protestant vicar said to George afterwards: 'I envied you while you were speaking: for you declared the gospel to the Roman Catholics, which they will not afford me the opportunity of doing.'

He returned again to Dublin and lectured on temperance at the Rotunda (where my maternal grandfather, Joseph Kidd, who later married his grand-daughter Frances Octavia, studied medicine a few years later). He also lectured on peace at a Methodist meeting in Abbey Street.

Around Belfast he had the use of a covered carriage to visit neighbouring towns, where he lectured on peace, moral reform and also to parents and young children of the 'labouring classes'. At Moyallan, his wealthy host was zealous in promoting the cause of temperance, and had instituted a loan-fund system for converts to total abstinence.

His labours in Ireland were now for the present closed after visits to Lurgan, Portadown, Armagh and Dungannon. By this time his son had so far obtained the approval of his kind employer that he was engaged as an apprentice on a mutual verbal obligation, which greatly pleased him.

George now received £100 from two individuals who remained anonymous, which allowed him to publish his second (1839) book. On leaving Ireland, he was aware that his son desired a watch, and he gave him his own. But at Liverpool, a lady saw that he was without a watch and presented him with another.

On his return home after 4 months in Ireland, he found that his wife had returned to animal food, on health advice. She wanted him to do the same, and he concluded that three and a half years abstinence was sufficiently taxing to his health.

His wife had long taken part in a benevolent institution formed to aid unhappy females who desired to desist from evil habits. She had encountered a Sergeant's wife, an Irish Catholic, who had been left behind while she gave birth to a baby daughter, when her husband was posted to Gibraltar. George found that a passage fee of £5 was needed and supplied this, assisting the lady to the steamer. He was later reimbursed of this advance by some 'disciples'. The Sergeant, a devout man, wrote to George expressing his extreme gratitude. This story of generosity on his part ends his second book.

There is no further record of George until 1841 and it must be assumed that his self instigated pilgrimages had taken its toll on his health; not only his abstinence from meats, but also his meagre diet of water and tea could not but have affected his constitution, even though all the evidence suggests that he was possessed of immense physical stamina. He reappears in Brazil in 1841, and was there for two years, so probably went there in 1840 and departed in 1841 or 1842.

23. Camden Street, Dublin, in 2009. There are quite a few Georgian buildings left there, as the view shows. George Pilkington may well have lived during his boyhood in a residence like those in the left foreground of this picture. St. Peter's church has been demolished, but its graveyard is preserved. (photo by Ian Sanders).

Table 4: Itinerary 17, Ireland

Town	Summary of details
Wicklow	14.11.1837 – 21.2.1838
Ferns	1756 miles: 42 towns
Enniscorthy	60 lectures on peace in 120 days: to 21500 persons: 1300 in temperance: 1000 on moral reform
Wexford	Parents and teachers addressed: 150
and on to ↓	**then** ↓
Waterford	Moate
Youghall	Clara
Cork	Tullamore
Fermoy	Edenderry
Clonmell	Belfast
Carlow	Bangor
Tullow	Lisburn
Goree	Carrickfergus
Arklow	Antrim
Kingston	Cotton Mount
Dublin	Holywood
Ballitore	Moyallan
Maryborough	Lurgan
Mountrath	Portadown
Roscrea	Tullylinch
Limerick	Banbridge
Ennis	Tanderagee
Galway	Armagh
Ballinasloe	Dungannon

25. 1841: A glimpse of George Pilkington in Brazil

All we have relating to this episode in his life is his address to the English residents in the Brazilian empire, urging them to give up slavery (and a suggestion by a Catholic priest that he adopt the Catholic faith). The 19 page document is held at the British Library. In his two years in Brazil he held public meetings in several provinces. We do not know whether he was supported there by the Anti Slavery Society or went on his own volition: the latter is unlikely, as he was very short of funds on leaving Ireland in 1838.

Whereas, there is a suggestion in the records of the Institute of Civil Engineers that he also did civil engineering projects there, this at first seems unlikely, as he would have been, and evidently was, extremely unpopular in a society riddled with slavery. A short article by Tony Murray in "Civil Engineering" published in 2007 suggests that he was unpopular with the local landowners because he was chiefly concerned with promoting the emancipation of slaves. He may well have been involved in small engineering projects related to the English landowning community there, as well as lecturing.

He commences with a counter to an argument 'that it is alright to tear away the relatives of unoffending Africans': he considers those who do this thieves and murderers. He then counters various arguments that slavery is condoned in the Old Testament and New Testament, very convincingly. He notes that if slaves fled to the Jews, the latter were forbidden to deliver them back to their masters, but had to find accommodation for them (Deuteromy 13: v15-16). He quotes various writings of the Apostles (e.g Timothy, Colossians, Hebrews, Philippians, James) and concludes that slave-owners are man-stealers. He thus rejects the Brazilian slave-owners' excuse that 'we have purchased our slaves, after they have passed through many hands; therefore we cannot be called man-stealers!

He quotes in passing the awful origins of slavery, from a writer named Buxton: the village is attacked in the night and set on fire to increase confusion: the wretched inhabitants are seized as they are flying naked from the flames, and carried off to slavery. He also quotes a narrative of one named Denham, citing one instance where 16,000 were carried away, 20,000 being killed. He does not pull any punches! The slaves were commonly secured while on passage by securing the right leg of one to the left of another slave in the same fetters, every four slaves being also secured by a twisted thong. They marched is this way through the heat, with little water supply. Denham reported that from 60 to 80 skeletons were left behind on such passages, each day!

Against this barbarity, George quotes the typical Brazilian housekeeper, who says 'I must have servants: if she did not purchase her one to six slaves, another would.'

He goes into the question that 'Brazilian law did not totally forbid slavery, so one should let well alone'. There is much more to his address, but the reader should read the full text; he ends by saying that he is sorry to so address his countrymen, many of whom are otherwise conducting their temporal affairs in a manner that commands respect. Despite this, we know that he had to flee from Brazil, because of the anger that he aroused.

A final point, one does not wish to enter into sectarian controversy (and God knows that the British were earlier deeply involved in slavery), but in the story of George Pilkington's fight against slavery, one cannot help noticing that the Catholic countries (especially Spain and Portugal) persisted with encouraging slavery, apparently reconciling it with their Christianity, long after George IV published the decree below - through William IV's reign, and even into Victoria's reign.

George IV's decree:

> *"Be it so enacted, that if any person shall deal or trade in, purchase, sell or barter or transfer, or contract for the dealing, trading in, purchase, sale, barter, or transfer of slaves, or persons intended to be dealt with as slaves, & c, in every such case, the person or persons offending, and all accessories, are declared to be felons, and liable to transportation for fourteen years, or imprisonment, and hard labour for five years, nor less than three years."*

....

26. The author's evaluation of George Pilkington's character: 150 years after his death

George Pilkington lived in a quite different age to our own 'Global Village' electronic age of the early 21st Century. He was brought up as a Protestant in Ireland, but was turned off religion by the horrors of the 1798 rising, which he experienced as a youth of 13 and in which he apparently saw awful perpetrations in the name of both religions. He was a 'deist' or 'atheist' until 1825, when he was 40 years old, a surprising fact, for he married Charlotte Clara Jollie, probably in St Bride's, Fleet Street, in 1816 (though another record states that it was at St. George's, Hanover Square). She was a devout Christian woman throughout her life.

He experienced a 'Pauline' conversion during a service at the Catholic chapel in Trinidad in 1825, swayed by Episcopal oratory. His religion thereafter was based on gospel reading and developed from this over his remaining five years employment as a civil engineer in Trinidad. His was a profession which works on accumulation and literal readings of facts, and he derived his religious precepts from literal reading of the gospels.

His antagonism to slavery was deep rooted and must have originated in his first, Napoleonic, service in the West Indies, where he would have seen slaves working in the plantations, but was strengthened by his extraordinary experiences in West Africa, from 1816-1820, where he saw the perfidy of both the indigenous slavery promoters and their European customers, in what has been called the 'partial revival of slavery' during these years, by countries other than Britain (see 'West African Sketches; F.T. Collier 1824). He was even rescued by a Spanish slave ship, and saw at first hand the appalling conditions under which the slaves were transported.

He was again unfortunate in that he fell between two stools in Trinidad, between the enlightened rule of Governor Ralph Woodford, who took over the former Spanish colony in 1813 and was trying to gently bring in changes in attitude to the 'coloured' settler population and Amerindians - the British colonists operated a rigid colour bar - and Governor Grant, who succeeded Woodford on his death in 1828, and totally ignored George IV's benevolent dictum, rather than bring down the ire of the British colonists on his head (conveniently George IV had died also by then). George Pilkington may have been very tactless to promote coloured people provisionally to officer rank, but he may have had more encouragement from Governor Woodford than we know of. He was then treated with extreme shabbiness by depriving him of his official emoluments and deliberately making him a pariah, so that he had, perforce, to leave Trinidad. In view of his excellent previous record alone, he should have been paid what was due to him and not left a penniless outcast on the streets of London, with a wife and four small children to feed.

He admits that his adoption of his extreme view on the lawlessness of any form of military service according to the gospel, even defending your wife and family, was something he picked up from someone else. He probably would never have adopted such an extreme view if, in Trinidad, his militia status and trappings as a Major had been preserved, together with his official Colonial Civil Engineer's appointment. He adopted what was a very unpopular stance. Probably, otherwise, he would have served on in Trinidad.

In the aftermath of the Napoleonic Wars, of which he himself was a survivor and one-time prisoner of war, such an extreme stance even made him unpopular with the Peace and Temperance Societies who employed him for a time, and possibly even with the Anti Slavery Society, though with them he does seem to have remained on good terms, after Government Legislation caused his employment with them as a lecturer to be terminated in 1832. They may even have sponsored him, in Brazil in 1840-1842, for he surely could not have found the funds to go there himself, unless he also had engineering work there, which has been suggested - but is exceedingly unlikely?

The big step he took was to go on a series of 'pilgrimages', like the Wesleys and Whitefield, on his own volition. In this he was popular with the disestablished church, the Friends, Methodists, Moravians etc, but clearly with only a minority of the established church and Catholics: unlike the Wesleys, he was not ordained, and he decided on this immense series of pilgrimages as a layman because he sincerely believed God had ordained it. In fact, he says that he declined an offer of employment in his profession at Birmingham in 1835, because of his belief that God still called him to preach and lecture throughout the land: though there is strong reason to believe that he later accepted it, and that work on the railways there fills the gaps in the record of his life from 1838-1840 and 1841-1848.

His pilgrimages were an immense undertaking, relying on entirely gifts to keep him and his family, to travel and to subsist meagrely. We can only guess why he suddenly abandoned this mode of life in 1842 after the Brazil venture, but he was clearly becoming exhausted in 1838 while in Ireland and irritated by dissent at his meetings there. He may even have combined some further lecturing with some professional work in England after 1838.

In relation to his pilgrimage years, one cannot question his sincerity. That is not to say that he was not without foibles. He believed God ordained that his 'disciples' should keep him in enough funds, while never letting him have too much. Yet he was against going to law in the case of Edwin, and one could equally say that God was ordaining the lawyer engaged by Catherine Watson to act in this good cause. He was selective – he selected tracts from the Old and New Testament that supported his contention regarding the total Christian interdict against even a defensive War. One could no doubt select other tracts that support the opposing view.

His pilgrimages were carried out during a remarkable period of years of peace, except in India: and he emigrated to South Africa before the 'Indian Mutiny' or 'Sepoy Rebellion' and Crimean War burst out. Some critics observed that it was pointless going to such lengths to lecture against even a defensive war in such a period of peace. Whether any of his children followed his precepts we do not know: Clara (my great-grandmother) married Robert Rouse who was a former Naval Lieutenant of Protestant/Liberal persuasion. Woodford became a civil engineer following George, and was very close to him, and may well have followed George's dicta about war. George William reappears in South Africa as a successful builder, and that he clearly honoured his father is evident from what he wrote on the Cathedral memorial in Cape Town. We can be certain that his wife, Charlotte, was with him all the way.

His grandson, George Mills, had a very distinguished military career, especially in World War 1, and the author himself, with six years of very undistinguished service (four overseas) in World War 2, remains convinced that you cannot just turn the other cheek when confronted by unmitigated evil such as was represented by Hitler and the Nazi Regime: the pictures of the piled bodies discovered at Belsen and Buchenwald still haunt me. Yet he admires extreme pacifists such as George and he believes that there should always be a voice for them in the world, even if, he willingly and with pride, served in a defensive war against evil. He himself was vigorously opposed to the recent Iraq war, which he believes was embarked on with the justification of fabricated evidence.

George at times was driven to absurdity by the extremeness of his views. He attributed the activities of the Ashantees to ill treatment by the British at Cape Coast. This was naïve? Collier, in the work quoted above, described the atrocities of human sacrifice by the then Ashantee ruler and the fact that in the early eighteen-twenties, in the 'partial revival of the slave trade', his one aim was to either gain access to the coast so as to drive his Buncatoo neighbours, a peaceable tribe, as slaves to the coast for embarkation. He thought the Danes might give him such access from Fort Elmina, but, failing this, mounted attacks on Cape Coast Castle. The description of the manner in which the slaves were transported to the coast, as described by George Pilkington in his Brazil address, is chilling.

There is no way these attacks can be simply attributed to mistreatment by the British at the coast and they were undoubtedly part of the wicked trade which George so valiantly opposed throughout his lectures and pilgrimages. Slavery operated because of two evil agencies - the plantation-owning Nations (including the British) in North and South America and the villainous African Kings and Chiefs. There would probably have been some slavery in West Africa without the impetus from the other side of the Atlantic

– slavery was a fertile business in East and Central Africa as well at the time, where the two evil agencies were the Arab traders, supplying mainly Asia, and the chiefs in the interior supplying the bodies.

His lectures were very long - 2 hours was the norm- and one can see the model from his splendid tract against slavery in Brazil published there in 1841, which is loaded with quotes from both testaments. The world of that time was much concerned with religious dissertation, in a way that the modern world is not. There was little entertainment in provincial towns, and the people welcomed preachers and lectures on religious and moral topics, and especially from people, like George, with wide experience of the outside world. Even the children apparently listened to him quietly for more than an hour at the time. He was certainly a very gifted orator, but of course the nature of his pilgrimages meant that he could repeat himself again and again.

George's contribution to the Edwin rescue was brave, self-sacrificing, and carried out without blemish. Particularly impressive is his feeling for the downtrodden Shetland islanders of the time and his contempt for the overweening minor gentry and lairds.

He had a good sense of humour, and told stories against himself: for example, falling off a very rascally Shetland pony! He criticised himself to a fault and was always on the lookout for being too proud of his achievements, and in this he had a reliable monitor in Charlotte, as he relates against himself more than once. Like a more famous Irishman (W.B. Yeats), he was 'silly like us!' The absurdity of the story he tells of a visit to Ipswich, where he got his conscience in a tangle about doffing his hat to some ladies in the street, and removing the same hat in a church service for the Almighty, is an instance of this: and he even apologised later to the same dumbfounded ladies for doing this! But despite his foibles he was a quite remarkable man. His physical achievements in his long pilgrimages alone must be unique – they are summarised in Table 5.

He can be criticised for long absences from his family, but there is little doubt that Charlotte was prepared to put up with this, as she believed in his mission. Going away at Christmas seems a bit obsessive, however.

In summary, though the author does not agree with his extreme view on war and peace, he finds him a quite remarkable man, of great moral courage, and for his Anti-slavery and colour prejudice stance and rescue of Edwin alone, merits nothing but praise. He was extremely unlucky three times – strangely the author himself had two such instances in his own career, encountering a paranoid and xenophobic superior while lecturing at a University, and two years later getting into the middle of an intra-company family quarrel, and he too overcame them, though they were not as calamitous as George's troubles. George Pilkington overcame his three major disasters with great courage, but with the support of some very generous friends and a remarkable wife.

His call by the Almighty to carry out his pilgrimages may be difficult to understand by those who like myself have never felt such a call, but the author was quite recently talking to a medical missionary for the CMS who in the 21st Century told him that he had felt just such a call to return to Kampala, after completing six years with his family in a remote part of Uganda: such calls are within the person concerned and are undoubtedly real.

The strangest thing of all is that after 1838 he returned to his profession and had a distinguished late career in it; this is described below after a chapter on how he became involved in my maternal ancestry.

Table 5: Summary of George Pilkington's preaching/lecturing over four years in the U.K.

Itinerary	Date	Miles	Towns	Lectures	Persons (peace)	Persons (temperance)	Children	Parents Teachers
Trial	April 1834	840	18	19	9,900	-	-	-
1st	13.6.1834	713	25	38	12,300	-	1,750	2,650
2nd	30.7.1834	453	38	30	15,880		1,130	1,760
3rd	10.9.1834	625	20	28	17,300	950	2,400	1,550
4th	5.11.1834	561	18	27	15,900	-	2,100	2,900
5th	8.12.1834	605	20	20	13,020	600	1,400	1,350
6th	4.2.1835	1,017	40	56	31,850	1,900	7,327	5,550
7th	7.5.1835	690	40	51	17,950	1,500	2,410	2,620
Scotland, Shetland	11.7.1835	1,508 (64)	8	9	6620	-	800	-
8th	15.10.1835	1,481	59	82	53,470	4,330	3,030	2,510
9th	1.3.1836	1,279	58	74	25,490	5,330	2,920	1,280
10th	19.8.1836	701	21	26	8,650	2,200	400	200
11th	17.10.1836	781	29	44	14,360	5,700	5,650	2,420
12th	20.12.1836	130	6	7	2,450	450	100	300
13th	20.2.1837	383	26	40	10,700	700	1,800	3,770
14th	13.4.1837	377	15	19	6,800	600	150	300
15th	20.6.1837	458	24	31	8,180	350	750	100
16th	8.8.1837	107	7	10	1,720	-	300	820
17th	14.11.1837 21-2.1838	1,756	42	60	21,500	1,300 (1000 moral reform)	-	150
Totals	1834-1838	14,565	514	671	294,040	26,910	34,517	30,230

He does not itemise talks on slavery, but this was presumably included in his Peace topic and in the later two years, 1840-1842, he gave lectures on slavery in Brazil. Whereas, the above tabulation covers entirely self-motivated 'pilgrimages', we do not know how he funded the later Brazil enterprise: when he finished Itinerary 17 in Ireland he certainly had inadequate funds for such an enterprise and it seems that he was probably funded by the Anti-Slavery Society or (most unlikely) combined engineering work with lecturing. Some of his figures are rounded off, but it is clear that as a trained engineer, he kept a log book of attendances and probably utilised an assistant to count the numbers.

....

27. The Rouse connection

There is a gap in the record of George Pilkington from 1841 when he engaged in a discussion with Brazil about the continuance of slavery, and the marriage of Clara Pilkington, his daughter, to Robert Rouse, at Islington in 1843, where it can be assumed George and Charlotte were still residing. This is where the author's ancestry from the Pilkington's originates. It is necessary, now, to go back to the origin of the Rouse's, which in itself is very interesting.

James Rouse (or Rous) was a Huguenot immigrant from France, probably Paris, born in 1756. He was a rope-maker, a very skilled profession, much in demand in the Navy, and came to Plymouth Docks to practice this trade. He has come down to us in a little painting, formerly the property of Sir Alexander Rouse, an engineer and the author's mother's cousin, held in the British Museum (probably now passed to the British Library). He married Sarah Palmer on 12 July 1778 at Stoke Damarel, Devon. They signed the register with a cross, and my mother assumes that they were illiterate (there was a lot of snobbery about this among the Rouse relations, which is absurd, and anyway the reason may have been that he spoke only French). He died in 1841.

His son was James Wood Rouse, who enlisted as an A.B., and lost a leg in the Battle of the Dardanelles in the attack on Prota under Admiral Duckworth in 1807. He was promoted in consequence to the rank of Lieutenant in 1807 and granted a pension of £91 5s from the Patriotic Fund. He served in this rank for 50 years, mainly as a naval instructor as First Lieutenant of the Royal Naval College at Portsmouth. He was finally admitted to Greenwich Hospital. He married Peggy Dunstone, a postmistress at Flushing, near Falmouth, where the packets landed their mail including bullion. Her likeness was also held by Sir Alexander Rouse, and is stored at the same place. The author possesses a copy of a colour portrait of James Wood Rouse.

His eldest son went to sea as a midshipman in the Navy in HMS Pallas in 1828 and I have his mother's letter to him on departure:

Mr Robert Rouse
H.M.Ship
Pallas
13.October 1828

My dear Robert

I hope to see you again before you sail. I cannot let your papa go without a few lines to assure you how very dear you are to us all, and to tell you nothing will ever change our affection but a change on your part, which that God may prevent is my most earnest Prayers – never forget my precious boy that his all seeing eye is ever on you, though you are surrounded with evil, and many temptations will be thrown in your way, if you look to your God for help be assured he will always preserve you from harm, but do not trust my dear boy to your own *strength for human nature is too frail to stand alone. He can only be your support in the day of trial, and for the sake of his beloved Son 'who has promised to feed his lambs' will do so. I will now leave this subject, hoping that with God helping you you will never forget what I have written and don't forget daily to look into your text book and read your bible as often as your time will permit – and I would say <u>never waste any time</u> for it is a precious talent given us to improve your keeping up your navigation and will be greatly to your advantage and please your Dear Papa and will give us both pleasure and this I feel satisfied you will be happy in doing, this steady line of conduct will make you many friends and we cannot get through the world without it – It appears uncertain where you are going or how long you will be absent, but should you want to draw on your papa your bill should not exceed £10-0-0 and at thirty days date, he has provided for four months mess with Lt Kelly so that in all probability you will return to Portsmouth before you want a supply – I need not beg you to observe economy for I have never observed any disposition in you to be extravagant – I shall make a parcel of your clean linen not having your bag, the little that remains dirty I shall retain that you may find a clean shirt on your return. The gingerbread and biscuits I hope you will find comfortable in your middle watch, don't be too generous at the beginning, I hope you will find your little indulgences will last all the cold winter nights and when you walk the deck remember that you have all the kind thoughts of a affectionate grandfather, tenderly attached sisters and a worthy father and mother and the good wishes of many kind friends. I shall now conclude begging you my dearest Robert never to omit writing by all opportunitys, should you be in line of direct communication with the packets, you may direct your letters to your Aunt Kitty, but this must depend on your own judgement.*

Dear Fanny is still mending, Margaret is gone to Portsmouth with Miss Packman (?), grandfather is amusing the little ones, but they all write (?) in most affectionate love to dear Robert and sincerely regret you not coming on shore again. God Bless You My Beloved Boy and be assured you have the affectionate prayers of your devoted mother.

Peggy Rouse

Robert was born in 1815 so he would have been only 13 years old when he went to sea. He was extremely homesick at sea and missed his sisters (Peggy had six children of whom four were girls, and she is reported to have sent two, of the same size, to church wearing a single glove between them!). A second son, John also went into the Navy and had a distinguished career. Robert had an interesting voyage visiting the West Indies, Newfoundland and India via Brazil, but was destined to serve nine years as a Midshipman, despite being chosen to display gunnery to King William IV. At the time, after the Napoleonic wars there were reportedly 4000 lieutenants in the Navy! He did get promotion to lieutenant in the end, but resigned it, due to what the author's mother referred to as 'conflicting loyalties'. This must have been in 1837, when he commenced his career as a colonial broker, civil engineer and railway builder. The conflicting loyalties must have involved the duties to his family, for his mother had died and his father was in failing health by that date.

His wife dying young, John Wood Rouse was led a dance by his four pretty daughters, who were much sought after by wood-be swains at Portsmouth and Greenwich, but made good marriages in the end, including one to a naval Captain and another to a naval surgeon.

Robert was 28 when he married Clara, and presumably by now well established in business. There is a record of Clara being away at a school at Chester in 1841 while George was in Brazil and Woodford, her younger brother at school in Surrey. This suggests that Charlotte and Augusta may have accompanied George to Brazil.

138

Some evidence suggests that Clara was born in Trinidad in 1828 so she was apparently only 15 when she married! However, the marriage documents give her presumed date of birth as 1826, and this is probably correct, for her brother Woodford was 3 years younger than her and reportedly born in Trinidad in 1829. So, at 15 or 17 at the most, she embarked on what was a highly successful marriage, and gave birth to five sons, nine daughters and one son in that order! The author's grandmother was Frances Octavia, the eighth child of this marriage. It remains to note that John Rouse stayed in the Navy and became the Secretary of Greenwich Hospital.

The author once met Clara Bell, Clara's eldest daughter, a formidable mother of nine, then aged 86: one of the other daughters, Augusta ('Gussie'), eloped at 38 to marry an Italian Professor, and gave birth to the author's cousin Eudora Gleave (née Campanella), whom he knew well both in Rome and later in Sydney.

So, in 1843, the rich genes of the Rouse's were combined with the equally rich genes of the Pilkington's. How the author's Kidd grandfather, Dr Joseph Kidd, from Limerick, the 17th child of a family of 20, at the age of 51, came to marry Frances Octavia Rouse, then aged 18, who bore him seven children to add to the eight by his deceased wife, Sophia Mackern is another story. Dorothy McCall (née Kidd) was the fourth issue of this second family and the author her seventh and youngest child, born when she was aged 39 in 1920.

Feminists may say that here only the male line has been described! However, the truth is that the author knows nothing about the female line Jollie, Palmer and Dunstone families, except that the latter (who worked with her elder sister, Kate, in her father's post office in the port of Flushing) claimed descent from Lord Protector

Somerset, who reportedly had a lot of unofficial issue! A fruitful line of research would be to go to Urney, Westmeath, and investigate the antecedents of George Pilkington's father, another George William, and his connection to the Lancashire family. The Pilkingtons of Westmeath were reportedly a powerful Protestant family at the time of the 1798 rebellion at Kilbeggan in the county, and it is possible that a reference in his second book to 'his unfortunate father' refers to some injuries that he may have suffered to his property at this time. He may have lost his property and had to move to Dublin? George's earlier reference to the 1798 rebellion may well indicate that he experienced it at close hand, in Westmeath, when 13 years old. The Pilkington's still manufacture tiles at Mullingar in Westmeath.

....

28. Ten years more to run under southern stars: 1848-1858

After his daughter Clara's marriage to Robert Rouse in 1843, when he was still living in Islington, as was Robert (though the latter soon moved to Greenwich), George Pilkington disappears from the London scene, and the author's first conclusion was that he had died. But this was far from the truth. He had yet another decade of rich experience in his already very full life. In fact, he emigrated to South Africa in 1848 as Chief Civil Engineer to the Colony!

This extraordinary switch from his lecturing on Slavery in Brazil, in 1840-2, back to his original profession may have several causes. The fact that he went to Brazil means that he must have been financially supported there; for he was still nearly penniless when he left Ireland in 1838. The Anti-Slavery Society may have supported him in Brazil, and he may have made some money from minor civil engineering commissions there. He may have intended to emigrate to there? Charlotte's cause in Chancery may have borne fruition. There may have been other sources of funds. We note that he was offered secure employment in Birmingham in 1835 and declined it, believing that the Lord wanted him to continue his pilgrimages: perhaps the offer was repeated. It is probable that after 1838 he worked again as an engineer.

It is difficult to see how he could have taken up such a senior position in South Africa, designing railways, bridges and harbours without renewed experience in England and the 1840's were the age of the railway boom. I note that in a report by him on the Cape Town/Paarl railway project, a report full of costing estimates which display a considerable knowledge of railway projects, he quotes again and again the 'Birmingham Railway'. There are several Birmingham Railways constructed in the 1830's-1840's, but the London-Birmingham line constructed by Stevenson which was commenced in 1837 would seem to fit the case best. The author's belief is that from the time he returned from Ireland in 1838, he did get involved in the Engineering work related to this project. He could only have been appointed to this task in South Africa if he had previous experience of railway construction. His Cape-Town/Paarl Railway report is highly professional and knowledgeable. Tony Murray, in an article about his life, published in 2007, notes that his middle years are unchronicled and that it is likely that he spent them on engineering works in Britain. All the indications are that they were railway projects.

A clue may also be found in the fact that Clara's bridegroom, in 1843, Robert Rouse, then 28, already several years out of the Navy, was a Colonial Railway Engineer and Financer. It seems highly probably that George, either before or after his trip to Brazil, and whatever the source of funding, was now better off financially and able to at last to re-enter his Civil Engineering profession. Possibly, Charlotte, a strong character, persuaded him that the time to finish with preaching and lecturing was now, for he was already 53 years old in 1838, and 58 in 1843. The fact that he had threats on his life while in Brazil may have been a factor. He was already showing signs of physical wear and tear in Ireland. It is an amazing turn round, but turn round he did.

Probably, then, the missing years, 1843-8, were spent in his profession, in England, and likely in the Railway industry. George was highly active in South Africa, where he replaced Charles Michell as Civil Engineer to Cape Colony in 1848 at the age of 63. His first task was to build the lighthouse on Cape Recife to Michell's design. He also designed the plans and sections for the northern breakwater at Port Natal, producing a scaled reference table for its solid content (this, however, was never built). His name is associated with the Great Brak River crossing between Mossel Bay and George in the South Cape. This, he designed it with 13 stone piers and 12 'floating' wooden decks spanning 20 feet each, a controversial design called 'theoretical' and, described as 'one that could not possibly work out', but which lasted until 1965, when a solid bridge replaced it! He also designed the famous Roeland Street Gaol, now the Cape Archives.

Above all, he laid out the route for the first Railway in the Cape, between Cape Town and Wellington and Paarl. He did the work on this in 1857-8 at the age of 72-3, shortly before he died. It was completed, by his son Woodford, after his death. He also surveyed a better route in Bain's Kloof, where a high bridge is named after him. His last work was to survey a route through du Toit's Kloof, but this was not completed for 80 years. He died suddenly at Green Point. He was succeeded after his death in 1858 by John Scott Tucker.

The Pilkingtons lived at Green Pont, near Cape Town, in a lovely site, with a house facing down to the sea. It is very pleasant to think of Charlotte, after all her trials in a long married life, ending her days in such peace and tranquillity.

We have a picture of George in old age surveying the railway route in a book by the author's Mother published in 1980. Charlotte came home in 1856 and visited her daughter Clara, who was expecting her eighth child, my grandmother, at the time, at Greenwich/Blackheath. She took the opportunity of an offer of a passage from a Ship's captain, and arrived unannounced by Hackney carriage, followed by a train of carts containing sandalwood boxes containing presents for the grandchildren that she had never seen (seven had been born by that time). She took a fancy to Robert Rouse Junior, Clara's eldest boy who was ten years old at the time, and took him back to South Africa for a holiday at Green Point, near Cape Town, and he went out with his 72 year old grandfather on the route survey.

They went up-country in a grand cavalcade for a survey lasting a fortnight of the future course of the railway. A bullock wagon was drawn by a team of sixteen, with two horses bringing up the rear. There was a crew of native 'boys' and each bullock had a name, to which it would obediently respond. They outspanned at night. They then crossed a river, the bullocks rushing the cart up the steep bank, and then camped there for two nights. The survey progressed with bundles of poles and red flags over hill and dale. Alas, one of the native assistants broke the theodolite, so they had to give up and return home. One hopes that George refrained from swearing according to his long established discipline!

Robert Junior came home by a British naval ship: alas, he was not to have a naval career like Robert Senior, he apparently was settled as a cotton broker, a rather dull occupation in life. He was not very successful at it, according to report.

24. James Rous or Rouse, Huguenot rope-spinner. A black and white copy of a colour portrait, held by Sir Alexander Rouse, Engineer, and passed to the British Museum (probably now held by the British Library). Copy in McCall family collection.

25. Lieut John Wood Rouse RN, the author's, great great grandfather, whose son Robert married Clara Pilkington in 1843. They had 15 children, the 8th being Frances Octavia, my maternal grandmother (copy of a picture obtained by Sir Patrick McCall, the author's brother, from an unknown source, possibly at Flushing, Cornwall: copy now in possession of the author).

James ROUS or ROUSE
Born: 1756 (cal)
Died: 1841
Occupation:
Rope-maker,
Plymouth Dock

MARRIED:
12th July 1778
in Stoke Demerel, Devon

Sarah PALMER
Born: 1761 (cal)

John Wood ROUSE
Born: 1785 (cal)
Died: 12th May 1857 in
Greenwich, Kent
Occupation:
Lieutenant, Royal Navy

MARRIED:
23rd October 1812
in Falmouth, Cornwall

Peggy DUNSTONE

Robert James ROUSE
Born: 1815 in Middleton, Sussex
Died: Q4 1884 in Bromley Reg.
District, Kent
Occupation:
Colonial broker / Civil engineer
Railway builder

MARRIED:
Q4 1843
in Islington, London

George W. PILKINGTON
of Urney, Westmeath

George PILKINGTON
Occupation: Engineer

Clara PILKINGTON
Born: 1828 in Trinidad,
West Indies
Died: 2nd January 1899 in
Bordighera, Italy

Charlotte JOLLIE

Frances Octavia ROUSE
('Fanny')
Born: 9th April 1857 in
Old Charlton, Kent
Died: 29th November 1940 in
Heathfield, Sussex

Frances Octavia Rouse
married Dr. Joseph Kidd of
Brooklands, Blackheath, a widower
with eight children in 1874. They
had seven children.
Dorothy McCall was the fourth,
born in 1881: she herself had 7
children.
Dr. Joe McCall was the seventh,
born in 1920.

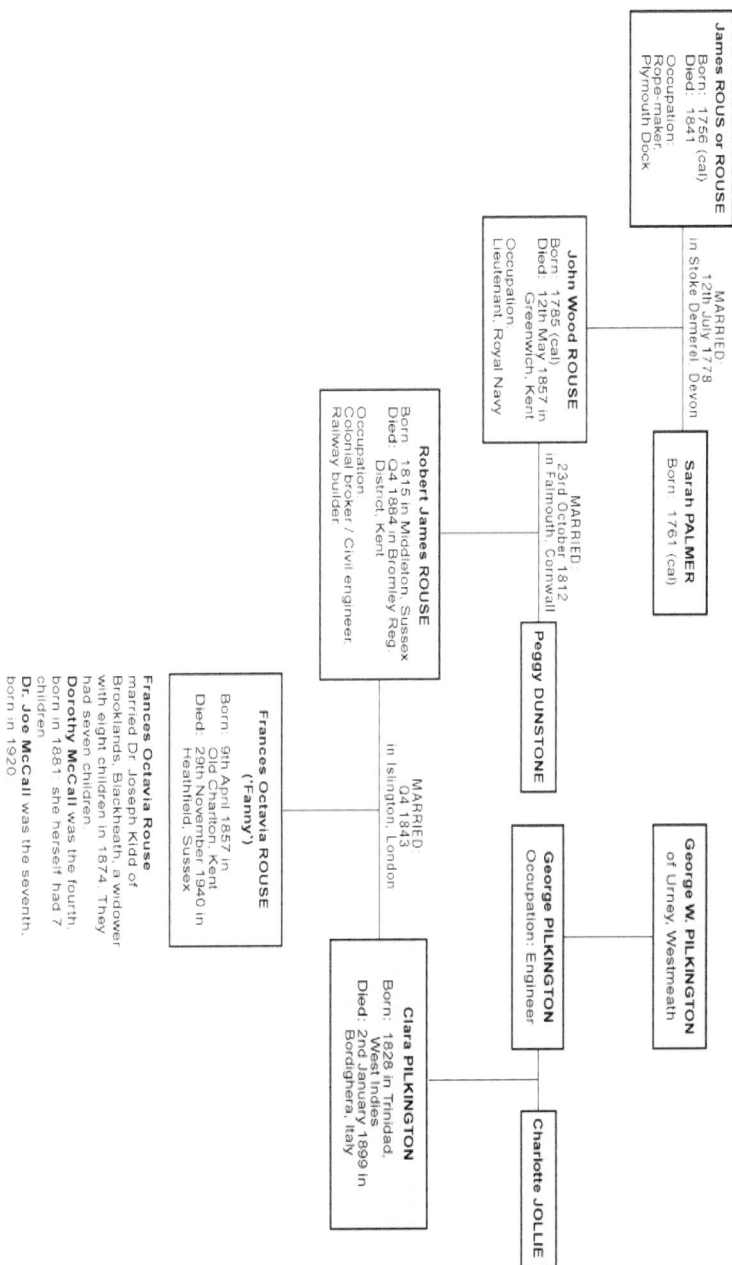

26. A family tree showing the Rouse and Pilkington
descent.

145

27. Cape Recife Lighthouse, just outside Port Elizabeth, South Africa, in Algoa Bay; built to a previous design by George Pilkington, it was commissioned in 1851 and is a 24 metre high masonry tower.

28. Pilkington's bridge at Great Brak Crossing. It was of pontoon design, much criticised, but lasted more than a century.

29. The Roeland Street Prison, Cape Town, designed by George Pilkington. It now houses Cape Archives.

Cape Town Station
André Kritzinger, 24 August 2003

30. The first line proposed was from Cape Town to Wellington, a short but important line of 45 miles that would serve the wine-growing districts of the Western Cape. The first sod on the construction of the line was turned on 31 March 1859, and the first trains in the Cape Colony started running on this line to Eerstrivier section in February 1862. The 0-4-2 locomotive used during construction was also used on the inaugural run when the Wellington line was finally opened in 1865. It was built in 1859 by Hawthorns of Leith, and is now serving as a station guard on Cape Town Station. This line was surveyed by George Pilkington, the survey completed by his son Woodford after his death in 1858.

147

29. Epilogue: The Pilkington 'Gene' yet flourishes

The author is aware that he has used the term 'gene' in an unscientific sense, quite differently from the rather arid story recounted in several books by Dawkins, which emphasise the role of the gene simply as a mechanism to ensure continuation of the species. We are familiar with families in which the same face reappears, remarkably through the generations, and part of the pleasure in tracing family antecedents, as the author has done, is to recognise certain character traits coming out again in descendents. He has used the term 'gene' colloquially to represent this. This extraordinary human race has developed in the last million years of the Earth's 4567 million years history, possessing the complex genetic system of other bio-organisms, and this genetic system ensures that, besides the dull continuation of the species, there is continuous change through breeding and mutation, and geniuses such as Bach, Beethoven, Handel, Sibelius, Dickens, and Yeats, appear form time to time and eccentric characters like George Pilkington and Martin Luther Rouse too: the descendents are all different. Here the author looks at the descendents of George Pilkington.

His mother describes George Pilkington as settling near Cape Town with his large family, and states that there are still a lot of the Pilkington name in South Africa. This was mystifying, because he apparently only had five natural children and one adopted son, his wife's orphan nephew, and the latter went to the Argentine, where two scapegrace Mackern relations of the author's Kidd grandfather were also sent, George and Hector Mackern. George William was apparently settled in Ireland and Woodford's family grew up in England, after he left South Africa. However, it is now known that George William had a family in South Africa.

The author has elucidated George's family history from the fog of doubtful dates: he married at St Bride's, Fleet Street (or St. George's, Hanover Square), in 1816, and they then went to West Africa. Charlotte was ill there and may have had miscarriages. They did not start a family until they reached Trinidad, when George was 37; there they had George William, Clara and Woodford. Augusta was born at Bideford in 1831. Charlotte Elizabeth was their youngest child, born ten years later, in Rio de Janeiro.

After completing this memoir, George William's later career was revealed, for his name was inscribed on the bronze memorial to George Pilkington in St. George's Cathedral, Cape Town. Diligent search of the 'world wide web' revealed the fact that he followed his father to South Africa in 1850. He worked as a builder in Cape Town, establishing the firm of Pilkington and McDonald in Castle Street. They built the Castle Causeway, the Customs House and the Standard Bank building. Born in 1822, he died in 1906. Another George William was born at Sea Point in 1879 and became a well-known artist in South Africa. He was probably a grandson, the son of one of George William's five offspring, for Woodford had long returned to England by then, and we know that Woodford had only two surviving offspring of his four, neither of whom had issue.

Clara we know all about; she had 15 children, Rouse's, and the line leads down to, Dorothy Kidd, and the author at the end of the line of six older siblings.

Woodford followed in his father's profession and completed his work in South Africa. He has an entry in the records of the Institute of Civil Engineers. He erected lighthouses at Bird Island and East London, also designing harbour works there. He was involved in road, bridge and railway construction in South Africa; also construction of a jetty at Mossel Bay. He was appointed Assistant

Colonial Engineer and Commissioner of Roads for the Colony. He developed plans to improve the depth of the Buffalo River, East London Harbour, but the work was haphazardly carried out. He designed Grey Hospital, King William's Town and the Native hospital there. He returned to England and worked as a consultant on Quebec and Boston harbours. His final position was resident engineer on the harbour at Ceara, Brazil. In 1889, he presented the National Gallery with the 'Admiration of the Shepherds' by G.B. Spinelli. His son Ralph died in an accident shortly after going to India as a young man. His daughter, Kathleen, never married.

The cryptic suggestion by Dorothy McCall that there are lots of descendents in South Africa named Pilkington is repeated by Tony Murray in his 2007 article – that there are many of his descendents in South Africa. It is probably true, but they must be all descendents of George William. Only in South Africa did the male Pilkington line from George survive.

Augusta married George Sexton Evans, an engineer, and they emigrated to Melbourne, Australia. She had eight children.

Charlotte Elizabeth married W. Downes Mills of Paddington, a cotton-broker. They had three offspring, the eldest being George Pilkington Mills, whom Charlotte gave birth to in 1867 and whom, like Kathleen, the author actually met in the 1930's. He was remarkable by any standard! He was born in Kensington and was associated with the Anfield and North Road Cycling Clubs. He first, in 1885, broke the record from Lands End to John O'Groats, a distance of about 900 miles, on a large-wheeled penny-farthing ('ordinary') cycle, in five days and ten hours. He reportedly just snatched sleep, no more than a wayside nod. The record still stands. He then broke the record on a tricycle. Each time he took more than a day off the existing record. He reportedly rode this route six times. He set records for 50 miles and 24 hours on penny-farthings and a tandem-tricycle record for 50 miles. He won the inaugural Bordeaux-Paris cycle race, and was accepted as an amateur after it (he was manager of a bicycle factory), when he proved that he paid all his expenses. He joined the army in 1889 and retired in 1906 as a major, but served in France as a Lieutenant Colonel from 1915-1917, being awarded the DSO and being three times mentioned in dispatches. He served in the Home Guard in WW2! He resided at times at Bathampton and Malvern, but died at Shirley, Surrey in 1945. He worked for a number of firms, Raleigh, Talbot, Aster and the Belsize Motor Company: also was director of the Small Arms and Machine Gun Department of the Ministry of Munitions (where my father also worked) in 1918.

George Mills can have had no compunction about military service, unlike his grandfather in his later years: yet he possessed the Pilkington 'gene' in two ways: extreme individualism and a quite remarkable physical constitution. The author remembers him as a rather stocky man of no great height, but extremely compact and well-built. He was very modest and quiet-spoken. The photo which we have of him seated on a tricycle shows him as rather lanky, but he was only 24 at the time and had filled out by the time the author met him.

The Pilkington 'gene' flourishes in Britain, but entirely in the female line from George Pilkington: the author knows of more than 100 descendents of Frances Octavia Rouse alone, Clara's eighth child, and Clara had fifteen children! Dorothy, Frances Octavia's daughter and the author's mother, with her seven, did her bit!

Strangely, the Pilkington 'gene' was far more evident in the author than in any of his six siblings: it evidenced itself in a really wonderful constitution which carried him, despite a severe genetic spinal malformation, through six years of very arduous but dull war-service in Madagascar and from Ethiopia to Tanzania in East

Africa: and afterwards through ten years of footslogging geological mapping in the Gregory and Kavirondo Rift Valleys of Kenya; in Western Australia; in Vanuatu and finally throughout the Makran Mountains of Southern Iran. Then, at the age of 60, he was employed for three years as chief geologist on a richly profitable gold mine in northern Quebec, regularly climbing up and down ladders underground!

He must also confess to recognising some similarity of the eccentricity of George Pilkington himself in his own character. He is not out of the ordinary box! Likewise, his two daughters, Bridget and Fiona, his son Chris, and his grandson Thomas are, he believes, well-endowed with the Pilkington 'gene'!

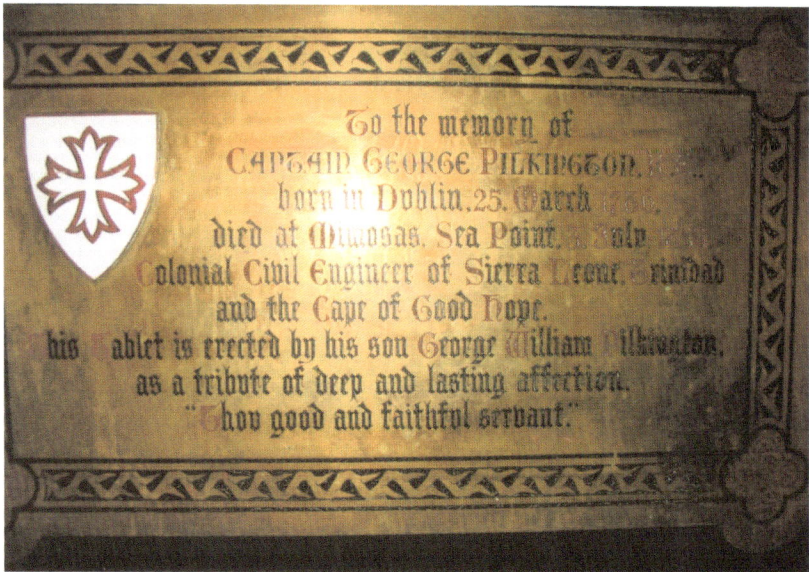

31. The memorial to Captain George Pilkington, RE, in the cathedral.
(photo Kathryn Harris).

32. George Pilkington Mills, his grandson by Charlotte Elizabeth Pilkington. Mills was the dominant British cyclist of his generation, establishing 19 separate records. He completed the Land's End to John O'Groats route 6 times, once by 'Ordinary' ('pennyfarthing'), twice on a 'Safety', twice on a tricycle and once on a tandem (with T.A. Edge). His triumph in the Bordeaux-Paris race 'probably remains the greatest single British cycling triumph on the continent'.

33. George Woodford Rouse – George Pilkington's grandson by Clara and Robert Rouse: he was Clara's second son and emigrated to New Zealand. Are there traits of George Pilkington in his rugged physiognomy?

153

34. Dr Joseph Kidd, the author's grandfather, who married Frances Octavia Rouse as his second wife at the age of 51. She was the eighth of fifteen children, the third of nine successive daughters of Clara

35. Frances Octavia Rouse, the author's grandmother, taken when she was about 35.

Acknowledgments

My distant cousin, Peter Kidd, first drew my attention to George Pilkington. I must also acknowledge the great help given to me by Wendy Cawthorne of the Geological Society Library, who has assisted me on countless scientific projects. Ian Sanders, of Trinity College, Dublin, kindly photographed Camden Street, and my dear friend and neighbour Kathryn Harris, while on a holiday in South Africa, photographed the memorial to George in St. Georges Cathedral, Cape Town, with the help of the verger, Eddie Esau. I am heavily indebted to David Spencer, without whose extensive knowledge of computerisation this book would not have been finalised for publication; and who worked extensively on it without payment; and also to his daughter Laura, who set the whole text for publication in as good English as my style of writing permitted. I am indebted to my long-term friends, Brian Marker and Alec Trendall, who read drafts, encouraged me and/or suggested improvements. Finally, there are my dear wife, Rosemary, who put up with Pilkington for many months (though she saw my activities in this respect as something of a 'King Charles's Head!) and my two beloved daughters, Bridget and Fiona, who likewise put up with my preoccupation with my extraordinary great-great-grandfather.

Please visit the website www.thepilkingtongene.com and leave a message in the Guest Book if you wish to contact me.

Sources of illustrations

1. Original, author
2. Original author
3. From 'Shetland isles'; T Cluness 1951. Robert Hale, London, 18 Bedford Square, London, end map
4. Original, author
5. Original, author
6. http://www.galen-frysinger.com/Caribbean/antigua07.jpg
7. http://www.portcities.org.uk/london/upload/img_400/PU21962.jpg
8. Original author

9. http://en.wikepedia.org/wki/Freetown (in public domain)
10. http://en.wikepedia.org/wki/Freetown (in public domain)
11. From 'Trade Castles and Forts of West Africa'; A.W.Lawrence. 1963. Johnathan Cape, London.
12. http://www.moxon.net/images/image.php?folder=ghana&image= cape_coast5.jpg
13. Original author
14. http://www.globosapiens.net/subapp_profiles/travel-picture.php2file_name=santo-ant...
15. Original author
16. http://en.wikipedia.org/wiki/File:Sao_tome_se.jpg
17. American School 18th C., New York Historical Society (detail of an illustration)
18. http://en.wikipedia.org/wiki/File:La_Rochelle_slave_ship_Le_Sa phor_1741.jpg (in public domain)
19. http://upward.wikimedia.org/wikipedia/en/3/37/Port_of_Spain_ Harbour_1890s.jpg (in public domain)
20. From 'Shetland isles'; T Cluness 1951. Robert Hale, London, 18 Bedford Square, London, opp p.208
21. From 'Shetland isles'; T Cluness 1951. Robert Hale, London, 18 Bedford Square, London, opp.p.64
22. From 'Shetland isles'; T Cluness 1951. Robert Hale, London, 18 Bedford Square, London,, opp.p.49
23. Photo taken for the author by Dr Ian Sanders of Trinity College.
24. Photo copy of original painting, in possession of author among family documents passed down to him.
25. Copy of original painting discovered by his late brother, Sir Patrick McCall, source unknown (probably Flushing, Cornwall); copy donated to the author by his brother.
26. Family tree prepared by Peter Kidd, added to by the author.
27. http://photos1.blogger.com/x/blogger/6247/3789/1600/323561/ Recife.jpg
28. From Murray, A. 2007. Civil Engineer, March issue. 'Pastmasters 9 &10'; pp 47-48.
29. http://www.tanap.net/library/images/archives/capetown_pand_g root.jpg
30. http://mysite.mweb.co.za/29/residents/grela/transnet01.jpg
31. Original photo, Kathryn Harris 2009.
32. http://www.randonneurs.bc.ca/history/photo-pages/an-alternative-form-of-long-distance-cycling_g-p-...
33. McCall family papers
34. McCall family papers
35. McCall family papers.

Bibliography

Adkins, R.& L. 2006. The war of all the oceans. Abacus, London 534 pp.

Anon 2008. The First Cape of Good Hope Railway. Cape of Good Hope – Postal History http://www.latenightengineer.com/capepostalhitory/Railway-Cape-Wellington.html

Anon 2008. South African Railway: A Brief History. http://orangemarmtrading.com/SA_Railway_History.html.

Anon 2008. Railways of Birmingham. http:/www.bgfl.org/bgfl/custom/resources_ftp/client_ftp/teacher/history/jm_jones/jmj.

Anon 2008. Greenwich Guide: Vanbrugh Castle. http://www.grenwich-guide.org.uk/vanbrugh.htm

Anon 2008. Maritime Greenwich: A World Heritage Site: Thames Art and Literature. http://www.portcities.org.uk/london/server/show/ConNarrative.63/ChapterId/1317/Ma...

Anon 2008 Military memorials in St George's Cathedral, Cape Town. The South African Military History Society. http://samilitaryhistory.org/volo11rl.html

Anon 2008 Earl of Balcarres. http://en.wikipedia.org/wiki/Earl_of_Balcarres

Anon 2008. George Pilkington Mills. http://en.wikipedia.org/wiki/George_Pilkington_Mills

Anon 2011. http://www.bainhouse.co.uk/pilkington%20family.htm

Birchall, D.2006. The early years of the Anfield Bicycle Club. http://www.anfieldbc.co.uk/history.html

Chrimes, M.M. (et al.) (eds.). 2008.Biographical Dictionary of Civil Engineering in Great Britain and Ireland. Thomas Telfor/ICE Vol.2 1830-1890; 624-625.

Collier, F.T. 1824. West African Sketches. L.B.Seeley, London; 273 pp.

'Ebenezer' 1837. The Earl of Balcarres and the Hon. Mr Lindsay: a narrative of the authentic facts connected with the detention of the brother of the Earl of Balcarres. Printed by E. Collins, Green Arbour Court, Old Bailey, London, 19 pp.

Kidd, P. http://www.manuscripts.org.uk/FamilyHistory/

Lawrence, A.W. 1963. Trade castles and forts of West Africa. Jonathan Cape, London; 388 pp.

McCall, D.M. 1952. When that I was. Faber and Faber, London; 248 pp.

McCall, D.M. 1960. A string of beads. Faber and Faber, London; 200 pp.

McCall, G.J.H. (unpublished autobiographical manuscript). Thank

God for Life (2 vols).

Moxon, M. 2008. Cape Coast Ghana..
http://www.moxon.net/ghana/cape_coast.html

Murray, A. 2007. Past masters 9 and 10: George Pilkington and Charels Davidson Bell. Civil Engineering (Sivili Enjeneereng) 15(3); 46-47.

Pilkington G. 1836. The doctrine of peculiar providence: illustrated and defended in biological reminiscences. Effingham Wilson, Royal Exchange, London; 318 pp.

Pilkington, G. 1839. Travels through the United Kingdom in promoting the cause of peace on Earth and goodwill towards men. Edmund Fry and Son, Bishopgate Street, London; 318 pp.

Pilkington, G. 1841. George Pilkington's reply to a priest, who by letter, kindly expressed the desire that he should adopt the Roman Catholic faith; 34 pp (held in British Library ref. 8180).

Pilkington, G. 1841. An address to the English residents in the Brazilian empire [Urging them to liberate their slaves] Laemert, Rio de Janeiro; 21pp.

Pilkington, G. 1857. Report on the proposed railway from Cape Town to the Paarl and Wellington, with branches to Malmesbury, via D'Urban to Wynberg, and to Stellenbosch. Printed in 1858 by Eyre and Spottiswoode, London.

SAR & Transnet History 2003. A South African Railway History. http://mysite.mweb.co.za/residents/grela/transnet01.jpg

Tankard, K. 2003. Woodford Pilkington's Harbour. Knowledge Africa com. http://www.knowledge4africa.co.za/eastlondon/port00.htm

Watry, M. 2004. The Vale Press. Oak Knoll Press and British Library; 266 pp.

Winchester, S. 2010. Atlantic. Harper Press; 498 pp

Permissions Record

For most of the illustrations used, permission to use was obtained from the copyright holders. However, in the case of a few, either no answer was received to a request to re-use or the copyright holder proved impossible to trace.